A History of
Human Resources

SHRM's 60-Year Journey

The Society for Human Resource Management (SHRM) is the world's largest professional association devoted to human resource management. Our mission is to serve the needs of HR professionals by providing the most current and comprehensive resources, and to advance the profession by promoting HR's essential, strategic role. Founded in 1948, SHRM represents members in over 140 countries, and has a network of more than 575 affiliated chapters in the United States, as well as offices in China and India. Visit SHRM at www.shrm.org.

ISBN: 9781586441418

Dedication

This book is dedicated to Susan R. Meisinger, SPHR, who devoted more than 20 years of leadership service to the Society for Human Resource Management and the HR profession.

During her tenure as President and CEO, Susan led SHRM through tremendous growth and seminal change. As a result of her efforts, the Society is successfully meeting the new challenges of a changing world by serving human resource professionals around the world and advancing the value of our profession.

SHRM and its 250,000 members are richer because of her vision, leadership and dedication.

Acknowledgements

This book was a result of a collection of efforts from many, many people. Kathy Compton, a former SHRM executive, spent months poring over boxes and boxes of SHRM Board minutes and other historical data to create a timeline of facts that formed the basis of this book. Writer Sharon Leonard, also a SHRM alumna, brought SHRM's history to life through her extensive knowledge of the Society and her eloquent choice of words.

The editor, David Narsavage, deserves special thanks for his keen eyes and creative flair. The SHRM Design & Production team, specifically Blair Wright, Jim McGinnis and Caroline Foster, created a beautiful design and layout under the most demanding deadlines. Madeline Delgado continually helped in times of need, locating photos, facts, dates and names from the last six decades. Frank Scanlan directed the project and kept everyone organized, calm, within budget and on time. And Bill Maroni, who oversaw this initiative, conceived of the original idea and format for this book as a commemorative account of SHRM's 60th anniversary.

Finally, a very special thank you to the thousands and thousands of HR professionals over the past 60 years who made this book possible by building a respected profession that has become an essential element of every organization's success.

Introduction

In the 60 years since the founding of the American Society for Personnel Administration—later renamed the Society for Human Resource Management—there has been monumental change in both the profile of business and the profession of managing human capital. Setting the roots for that change took nearly as long.

As the United States entered the 20th century, the concept of managing personnel was not yet born, and the life of an average working person was less than pleasant. In 1900, six out of 10 families were near poverty. Most families earned $500 a year—the equivalent of about $12,000 today. And the comparatively few women who worked made as little as $52 per year—$650 in today's money—for a 50-hour workweek.

It wasn't until World War I, and the labor shortages it created, that employers started looking more seriously at the issues of personnel management. The phrase "personnel administration" was created. But with the end of the war, the growth of the profession stalled and even reversed. On the eve of the Great Depression, most personnel policies in American industry looked no different than they did in 1900.

Then, with World War II and the growth of American industry, the fledgling HR profession emerged as a critical element in business, and there would be no looking back. Personnel directors from across the country began communicating about the need for a national organization that could help them develop professionally and promote their importance to the success of their organizations.

The American Society for Personnel Administration was born in 1948, attracting 67 people to its first annual meeting. Some years later, on September 1, 1989, ASPA changed its name to the Society for Human Resource Management, or SHRM.

Today, SHRM is the world's largest organization devoted to human resource management, with 250,000 members in more than 140 countries. It has more than 575 affiliated chapters, as well as offices in China and India. It is among the largest professional associations in the United States, and in 2006 the American Society of Association Executives named SHRM as one of the nation's seven best associations.

What hasn't changed in 60 years is the organization's dedication to serving the HR professional and advancing the HR profession. Not only does SHRM give its members the tools they need to succeed and grow in their role as HR professionals, it also spreads the word about the vital role that HR plays in the success of businesses everywhere. Today, SHRM is cited or quoted in thousands of news articles around the globe every year. The Society has truly become the voice of HR.

Contemporary HR professionals are expanding their skills and specializations in order to meet the demands of a rapidly changing workplace. Whether it's tapping the power of cultural diversity, recruiting and retaining the best talent around the globe, boosting productivity, or managing the rising costs of a broad palette of employee benefits—today's professionals face challenges that their predecessors could not have even imagined in 1948.

To help the professional meet those challenges, SHRM continually expands its member resources and its reach across the world. To better prepare professionals needed for the next 60 years, it develops curriculum templates and other teaching materials to raise the standards of HR degree content through specific educational requirements. Already, more than two dozen colleges and universities have adopted the SHRM HR curriculum.

Just like its founders who pursued a vision of an unprecedented national organization in 1948, SHRM's members today are truly involved and are enthusiastic supporters of their profession. In 2007 alone, they sent nearly 60,000 letters to lawmakers in Washington, expressing their opinions on key HR public policy issues, such as health care, immigration and family leave policies.

And, since lawmakers know SHRM represents nearly a quarter-million well-informed professionals on the front lines of workplace issues in every industry and sector, they listen. They listen when SHRM talks about critical public policy topics like health care, retirement security, family and medical leave, and workforce readiness. They listen because they know SHRM members speak for the needs of both employers and employees.

Unlike 60 years ago, when "personnel administration" was a secondary function, today HR is at the highest levels of management. C-suite executives look to SHRM members for the answers on meeting workforce needs for tomorrow, on recruiting and retaining global talent, on succession planning, on managing rising health care costs, and much more. That expertise is also becoming credentialed: SHRM's affiliate, the HR Certification Institute, celebrates its 30th anniversary this year. Nearly 100,000 HR professionals have been certified as PHR, SPHR or GPHR.

For the HR professional, it has been a remarkable journey from 1948 to 2008. Virtually every aspect of the workplace has changed, as have the boundaries of the marketplace. Such rapid evolution may presage even more dramatic change in just the next few decades. Those professionals with the many resources of SHRM at their side are ready—and eager for the challenge.

Contents

chapter

1940s

one

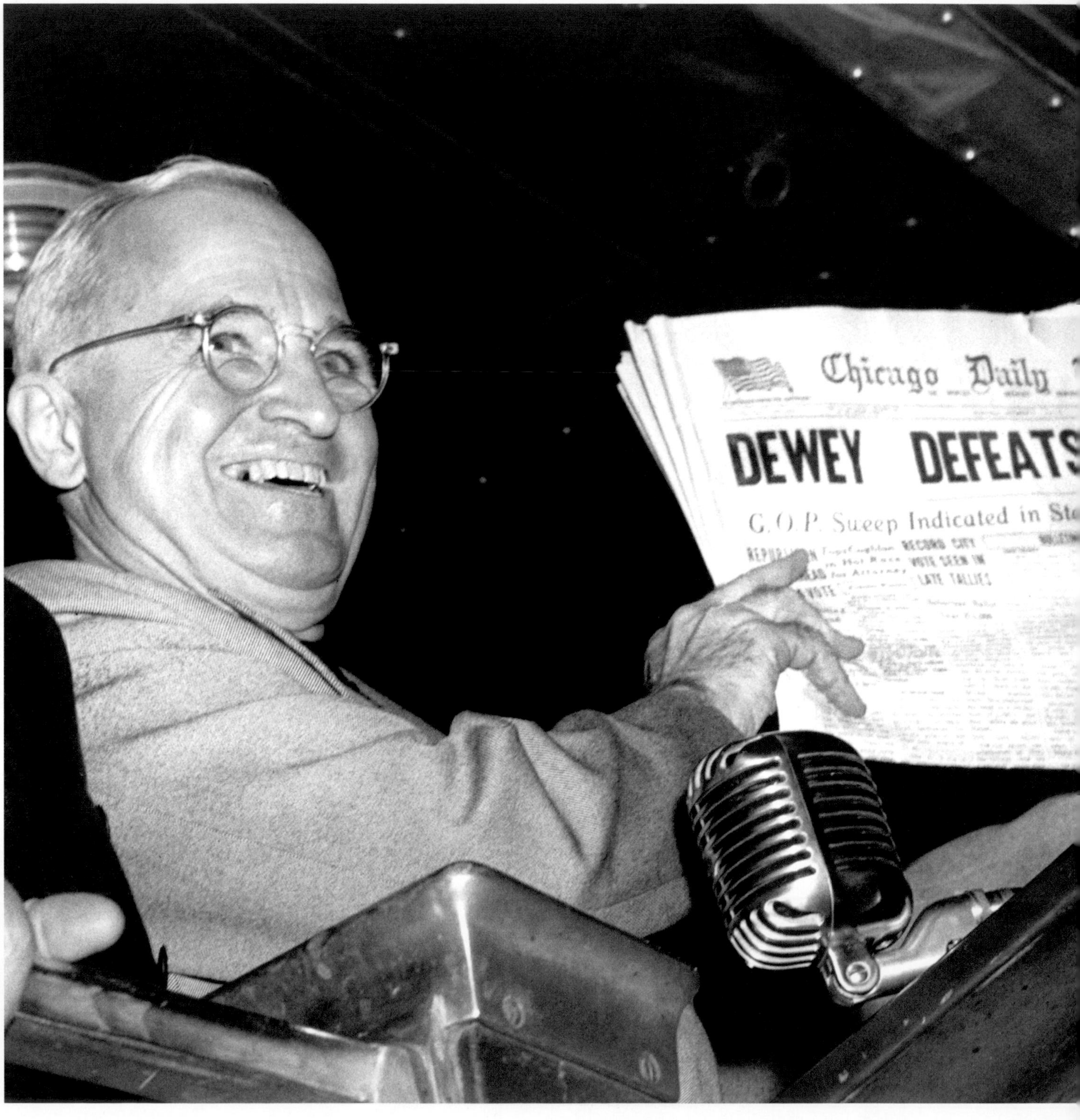

Personnel Administration: **The Seeds of a Profession**

In 1954, management guru Peter Drucker wrote in his book *The Practice of Management* that "a manager's task is to make the strengths of people effective and their weaknesses irrelevant." Today, Drucker is regarded as a visionary, but in the 1950s his ideas were considered revolutionary. When looking at the history of labor relations in the United States, his writings were revolutionary as well.

At the beginning of the 20th century, 18 million of the 29 million working Americans made an annual wage of about $500, which was actually less than the cost of living for a family of four (in 1900, U.S. families averaged 5.6 people). The workforce included 1.75 million children between the ages of 10 and 15 and more than 5 million women, many of whom worked for as little as 10 cents for a 10-hour day.

The U.S. was emerging as an industrialized society in the late 1800s, and the concept of managing employees was not just alien—it simply did not exist. Personnel or industrial relations departments were nonexistent. Most employment decisions were in the hands of first-line supervisors, the foremen. There was a general disregard for health and safety in the workplace, child labor practices were abysmal, and other abuses were commonplace. In addition, high immigration rates and low skill levels meant that there was an abundant supply of cheap labor, making early unionization attempts ineffective. In 1900, only 917,000 U.S. workers belonged to a union—or approximately 6 percent of the private-sector workforce.

Still, the seeds of what would become the human resource management profession were being sown. Employment agents and employment clerks, the people responsible for selecting the daily help, emerged at this time, while a few hiring halls and hiring offices were in operation. And in 1903, the U.S. Congress created the Department of Commerce and Labor, a sure sign that the management of people was becoming more important, not just in offices and factories but also at the government level as well. By establishing the department, Congress extended the federal government's authority to control interstate commerce and to monitor labor relations.

In 1909, Frederick W. Taylor wrote *The Principles of Scientific Management*. In his book, Taylor stated that the methods of work and management could and should be improved. He argued that businesses should find the right jobs for the right workers and then pay workers for increased productivity, not just for the jobs they performed. His ideas were groundbreaking, but most employers still left foremen in control of hiring, firing, training and paying workers.

U.S. President Harry S. Truman holds up an Election Day edition of the Chicago Daily Tribune, which, based on early results, mistakenly announced "Dewey Defeats Truman" on November 4, 1948. (AP Photo/Byron Rollins)

By 1920, there was a growing interest in labor relations, and Taylor's notion of "the right man for the right job" became a well-known mantra. Labor shortages and worker unrest led some employers to establish personnel departments. State and federal governments also became more involved in workplace issues.

In 1912, Massachusetts adopted the country's first minimum wage law. Because lawmakers worried that the law might be challenged as a violation of the 14th Amendment, they applied it only to women and minors and did not make it mandatory. Even though the Massachusetts law lacked teeth, it set a precedent that other states followed. Utah, Oregon, Washington, Minnesota, Nebraska, Wisconsin, California and Colorado enacted minimum wage laws in 1913. Arkansas and Kansas followed suit in 1915. Arizona enacted a minimum wage law in 1917, the District of Columbia in 1918, and Texas, North Dakota and Puerto Rico in 1919.

In 1913, the U.S. Congress created the Department of Labor, making it independent from the Commerce Department. The newly formed department included the Bureau of Labor Statistics, the Bureau of Immigration and Naturalization, and the Children's Bureau. In 1914, the Clayton Act limited the use of injunctions in labor disputes and legalized picketing and other organized labor activities.

The great catalyst for growth in the fledgling HR profession was the labor challenges employers faced during World War I. Because of the war, immigration slowed drastically, reducing a valuable labor source for U.S. manufacturers. While the demand to increase industrial output to support the war effort did create more jobs, the increase in job opportunities led to a spike in worker turnover.

The growing turnover, combined with the huge number of young men entering the military and the increased industrial output to supply the war effort, led to a severe labor shortage—the likes of which U.S. employers had never experienced. The labor shortage forced employers to raise wages to keep workers on the job and to improve the productivity of those workers.

In July 1917, the federal government established the War Industries Board (WIB) to encourage the creation of centralized employment departments in government-run industries and to create training programs for employment managers. The WIB encouraged employers to recognize unions, engage in collective bargaining, and improve the employer-employee relationship as a way to minimize strikes and production disruptions. The WIB was short-lived—it was decommissioned by executive order in 1919—but the agency had a powerful impact.

Between 1915 and 1920, the number of large U.S. employers (those with more than 250 employees) with personnel departments increased from 5 percent to 25 percent. This rapid growth seemingly created a new profession overnight; 500 people attended a national conference of personnel managers in 1917, and nearly 3,000 people participated in another national conference held in 1920. By then, the term "personnel administration" had been accepted by some, at least, as the name for the range of activities dealing with the management of laborers.

Issues surrounding the management of workers were gaining more attention around the world as well. In 1919, the International Labor Organization was formed as part of the Treaty of Versailles, the treaty to end World War I.

The early 20th century saw changes in the workplace, including child labor laws, the five-day workweek and improved working conditions for women.

In October that same year, the first International Labor Conference was held in Washington, D.C. During that conference, six international labor conventions were drafted and adopted. The conventions addressed hours of work, unemployment, maternity protection and night work for women, and minimum age and night work for young people. Despite these conventions, poor working conditions continued, and in the U.S., the subpar conditions led to widespread strikes and unrest.

The first U.S. child labor law was enacted in 1916. However, the Supreme Court found the law unconstitutional because it overstepped the government's powers to regulate interstate commerce. The law would have banned the sale of products from any factory or shop that employed children under the age of 14, from any mine that employed children under the age of 16, and from businesses that employed anyone under the age of 16 who worked night shifts or more than eight hours a day.

By 1920, other societal changes were becoming evident. A five-day workweek was adopted in the U.S., and voting rights were extended to women. That year, the Department of Labor added the Women's Bureau (still operating today) to develop and create standards and policies that promoted better working conditions for women.

The personnel profession's rapid growth came to an abrupt halt when World War I ended. As the war drew to a close, the forces that had driven the formation of personnel departments subsided. As soldiers returned home and the labor shortage eased, labor unrest decreased and the government loosened its wartime regulations on businesses. Organizations that had created personnel departments during the war now cut their budgets and let their programs lapse. Businesses that had never created personnel departments felt no compunction to establish them. By the mid-1920s, only 243 U.S. employers maintained active pension plans and only 399 had unions. On the eve of the Great Depression, American industry was made up primarily of organizations with personnel policies that looked much the same as they did in 1900.

Even though it appeared that little in the workplace had changed, the shifting attitudes about how workers should be handled were seeping into all areas of management.

Classic economic theory saw workers as instruments of production and subject to the laws of supply and demand. Industrial relations did not earn a place in economic and management theory until the late 1920s, when Elton Mayo, a Harvard Business School professor, studied productivity at Western Electric Company's Hawthorne Works in Chicago. Mayo's study concluded that simply being chosen to participate in the study improved worker productivity (called the "Hawthorne effect"). Mayo became the first scholar to show that workers respond to psychological stimuli. He performed experiments from 1927 to 1932 and discovered a principle of human motivation that revolutionized the theory and practice of management. Mayo's work brought about the human relations school of management that is still in use today in various forms.

Employers, though, struggled with the issues that the Depression created, especially unemployment and layoffs. In the *History and Development of HRM* (1933), economist William Leiserson wrote that "the Depression has undone fifteen years or so of good personnel work," and he warned that "labor is going to look to legislation and not to personnel management for a solution to the unemployment problem."

Leiserson's prediction was coming true. The Norris-LaGuardia Act (1932), the National Industrial Recovery Act (1933) and the National Labor Relations (Wagner) Act (1935) not only recognized the right of unions to exist but also promoted their extension, thereby legislatively setting in motion the resurgence of the personnel administration movement. These New Deal laws were rooted in the belief that there was an unequal and adversarial employment relationship between employees and employers that resulted in poor treatment of workers and employers' opposition to organized labor. To bolster employee morale and stall unionization, personnel departments tried to shrink foremen's power by making labor allocation (hiring, promotion, layoffs, dismissals) subject to precise rules and procedures such as seniority provisions, merit ratings, job evaluations, wage classification and progressive discipline.

The Wagner Act of 1935 protected workers' rights to organize and elect representatives for collective bargaining purposes. The Social Security Act of 1935 created a national social insurance system for workers and their families, provided retirement benefits, ensured benefits for victims of industrial accidents, established unemployment insurance, and offered assistance for dependent mothers, children and those with physical disabilities. That same year, union leader John L. Lewis and eight colleagues broke away from the American Federation of Labor (AFL) and formed the Committee of Industrial Organizations, later renamed the Congress of Industrial Organizations (CIO). Between 1936 and 1939, nearly 5 million workers joined unions.

In 1938, the Fair Labor Standards Act (FLSA) established a national minimum wage of 25 cents per hour, set the maximum hours for a workweek and defined a new set of child labor standards. According to officials in the Roosevelt administration, the FLSA was enacted to eliminate "labor conditions detrimental to the maintenance of the minimum standards of living necessary for health, efficiency and well-being of workers." Touted by President Franklin D. Roosevelt as "the most far-reaching, far-sighted program for the benefit of workers ever adopted," the FLSA was amended so that by 1945, the standard workweek was set at 40 hours and the minimum wage was 40 cents per hour. Nearly 700,000 workers were affected by the wage increase. Thirteen million more workers were ultimately affected by the work-hours provision, although the law did not include protections for African-Americans working in agricultural and the domestic fields.

During this time, the personnel profession was becoming more involved in management functions. Corporate personnel departments began setting formal and written procedures for hiring, promotions and layoffs. Increased unionization led personnel departments to create employee handbooks and corporate conduct codes. Unions also compelled personnel departments to develop discipline and dismissal procedures.

Between 1939 and 1943, Abraham Maslow published his work on the hierarchy of basic human needs of physiological safety, love, esteem and self-actualization. He believed that every person must meet each basic need before reaching self-actualization. His hierarchy quickly worked its way into management theory and practice and has had far-reaching effects on the world of work and the management of workers.

Despite the Great Depression, the young personnel industry was taking steps to keep Americans working while managing the growing adversarial relationship between management and labor.

The U.S. government had learned valuable lessons during World War I, and at the start of World War II it took an active role to prevent strikes from disrupting vital war industries. At the same time, unions were becoming more powerful. The combination resulted in a massive expansion of the personnel function.

By 1944, union membership had grown to more than 12 million workers, and as World War II drew to a close, nearly 34 percent of U.S. workers were union members. Unions were deeply entrenched in the major business sectors and demanded management's attention.

At the same time, the government became a permanent fixture in the workplace through its efforts to supervise union-management relations, restrain wage inflation, and regulate welfare benefits such as pensions and health insurance. Employers discovered they now needed specialized staff who could manage labor relations and ensure that their businesses complied with the new and very complex federal workplace laws enacted during FDR's New Deal.

As World War II ended, employers began to understand that there were economic benefits to treating employees fairly. Employers who did so developed good reputations in the marketplace and were more likely to be perceived as legitimate and responsible businesses (*Industrial Relations to Human Resources and Beyond, The Evolving Process of Employee Relations Management*, Kaufman et al., 2003).

Post-World War II: Personnel Administration

On December 5, 1946, President Harry Truman created the Committee on Civil Rights. The committee, chaired by C.E. Wilson, president of General Electric, was charged with proposing measures to strengthen and safeguard Americans' civil rights. The committee published its report *To Secure These Rights* in December of the next year. The report recommended that the federal government expand the civil rights division of the Department of Justice

The U.S. Between 1945 and 1960

- The gross national product (GNP) nearly doubled. From 1950 to 1960, GNP grew at an annual rate of 3.2 percent.
- Inflation remained less than 2 percent annually throughout the 1950s.
- The U.S. had a virtual monopoly over international trade.
- Because of technological innovations, productivity increased by 45 percent between 1945 and 1955. Auto production increased from 2 million in 1946 to 8 million in 1955, giving birth to suburbia.
- The American population grew by nearly 30 percent, mostly in urban and suburban areas. Home ownership grew by 50 percent.
- The middle class in 1947 was 5.7 million strong. By the early 1960s, the middle class had reached 12 million.
- By 1960, white-collar jobs were more prevalent than blue-collar jobs.
- Between 1940 and 1960, the number of farmworkers decreased from 9 million to 5.2 million.
- In 1946, approximately 7,000 television sets were in American homes. By 1960, there were 50 million.
- With the introduction of credit cards, consumer credit increased by 800 percent between 1945 and 1957.
- William Levitt pioneered mass-produced housing developments when he built 10,600 homes on Long Island in 1947. The area became known as Levittown—and is recognized as the prototype of all suburban developments.
- In 1940, less than half of the population belonged to a church. By 1960, that figure rose to 65 percent.
- College enrollment in the United States increased by 400 percent between 1945 and 1970.

and establish a permanent Commission on Civil Rights. It also recommended that Congress pass laws against lynching and to stop voting discrimination, and it suggested a new set of laws to stop racial discrimination in jobs. Congress did not act on the committee's recommendations.

A country tired of war and economic instability could not seem to find much peace. In March 1946, Winston Churchill made his famous speech at Westminster College in Fulton, Mo., where he coined the term "Iron Curtain" to describe the growing division between Western allies and the Soviet Union. President Truman declared a policy of intervention abroad and militarization of the economy at home. The Cold War had begun.

Communism was spreading beyond Soviet borders. In 1948, Czechoslovakia ousted noncommunists from its government and established its own rule. That same year, the Soviet Union blockaded Berlin. In addition, there was a general wave of anti-imperial insurrection in the world, notably in China, Korea, Indochina and the Philippines, most of which involved local communist movements. In reaction, anti-communism sentiment swept through the U.S.; between 1947 and 1952, 6.6 million people would be investigated under Executive Order 9835 to seek out the "infiltration of disloyal persons" in the U.S.

Through all the turmoil of the post-war world, Congress continued to involve itself in the workplace. The Employment Act of 1946 declared the U.S. government's commitment to maximum employment. Organized labor continued to wield great power; in 1946, a number of strikes took place around the country, including a United Auto Workers strike at General Motors and a steelworkers' strike at U.S. Steel.

There were also strikes abroad. In Africa, 100,000 gold mine workers went on strike for better pay.

In 1947, the Taft-Hartley Act, otherwise known as the Labor-Management Relations Act, was passed to control the power of unions. It amended the Wagner Act and made "closed shops" illegal. This meant labor unions could no longer force employers to hire union-only members, although the law did allow "union shops" where new employees could be required to join the union. The new law also established an 80-day cooling-off period for strikers in key industries, ended the requirement that employers collect dues for unions, forbade secondary boycotts and jurisdictional strikes, and required an anti-communist oath from union officers.

During this time, the U.S. began to address racial discrimination. In two landmark decisions, *Ada Lois Sipuel vs. Board of Regents* (1948) and *Sweatt vs. Painter* (1950), the Supreme Court ruled that African-Americans should be allowed to attend law schools in Oklahoma and Texas. In the late 1940s, President Truman issued executive orders banning racial discrimination in federal hiring practices and requiring the armed forces to institute policies of racial equality "as rapidly as possible." It ultimately took more than 10 years to completely desegregate the U.S. military.

1948 WORLD EVENTS

- Harry Truman is re-elected president of the U.S.
- President Truman abolishes racial segregation in the military.
- The cost of a new home averages $7,700, and a new car about $1,230.
- Workers' compensation laws are passed in all 48 states.

- Swiss outdoorsman George de Mestral invents Velcro.
- Scrabble is introduced.
- Popular movies: *Hamlet*, *The Red Shoes*, *Fort Apache*.
- Popular songs: *Buttons and Bows*, *I'm Looking Over a Four Leaf Clover*, *Nature Boy*.
- Popular TV shows: *Howdy Doody*, *Philco Television Playhouse*, *Meet the Press*.
- Popular books: *The Naked and the Dead*, Norman Mailer; *East Side, West Side*, Marcia Davenport; *The Ides of March*, Thornton Wilder.
- Average annual U.S. household income: $2,936.
- The American Society for Personnel Administration (ASPA) is founded.

The Architects of ASPA: **Planting the Seeds**

When the American Society for Personnel Administration (ASPA) was founded in 1948, workforce issues were becoming increasingly important. Hundreds of thousands of soldiers had recently returned home from World War II, and employers were scrambling to reintegrate them into the civilian workforce while simultaneously trying to adjust to a peacetime, Cold War economy. Workers' compensation laws were passed in all 48 states, while the massive power of the unions was generating a backlash. A perception that unions had too much power was growing among Americans.

The combination of these issues and explosive growth of U.S. industries boosted the growth of the personnel administration profession. The leaders of the burgeoning profession realized that the time had come for a national association that recognized and promoted the interests of practitioners. Since the early 1940s, the National

Association of Personnel Directors (NAPD), headquartered in Chicago, had tried to fill the void, but it was "pretty much a diploma mill," according to one ASPA founding member. Anyone who sent $50 to the organization would receive a document stating that he or she was a certified personnel director.

Personnel managers were "literally starved for information," said Mary E. Hopkins, SPHR, a retired management professor and the only female founding member of ASPA. "We grabbed at anything we could find, and that's why we had an interest in NAPD." But many NAPD members had serious concerns about the organization.

In 1947, a group of personnel professionals gathered in Chicago to attend the second annual NAPD conference. Leonard J. Smith, SPHR, a personnel director at the time, agreed to serve as co-chairman of the conference. When he arrived in Chicago, Smith and another volunteer, Russell Moberly, SPHR, a management professor at Marquette University, visited the NAPD offices and were disturbed by the location and condition of its headquarters as well as its lack of financial controls. After returning to their hotel, Smith and Moberly called a meeting to discuss their concerns. Nearly 30 people attended the meeting and formed an advisory committee to review the future of the NAPD and the personnel profession.

The advisory committee reviewed the NAPD's financial statements and declared them "untenable." When Hopkins showed the financial statements to her employer's attorney, "he recommended that we completely disassociate ourselves from this group," she recalled. "He also suggested that we consider forming a new association,

The ASPA logo is developed.

2917-23 East 79th Street,
Cleveland 4, Ohio

Purpose: To advance and develop personnel
ethics, methods and research toward
higher standards of performance leading to
the professional recognition of personnel
administration.

Membership
1. Member—a person professionally engaged
   in personnel administration, presently in an
   administrative capacity with at least three
   years of experience in responsible personnel
   work.

2. Associate member—Others who are
   believed by the membership committee
   to have a bona fide interest in personnel
   work and the purpose of the Society. Such
   members may not hold office.

3. Student member—Students in colleges or
   other equivalent educational institutions who
   are juniors, seniors or graduate students and
   who have a bona fide interest in personnel
   work with the purposes of the Society.
   Student members shall have no vote and
   may not hold office.

Applicants for membership must be sponsored
by a current member.

and I think everyone else on the advisory committee was coming to that same conclusion."

Before the advisory group could reconvene and present its final recommendations, however, the NAPD filed for bankruptcy in February 1948, effectively forcing the advisory committee's hand. (According to one account documented by David Cherrington and Bill Leonard in a 1993 article on the history of the Human Resource Certification Institute, the NAPD folded after it was revealed that the executive director was a convicted forger and that he had a questionable romantic relationship with the association's secretary/treasurer.)

In April, the committee recommended forming a new national organization and held meetings in New York City, Cleveland and Chicago to assess interest in the association. The advisory committee was not the only group interested in establishing a new national society; a number of other independent groups were looking to organize a new association as well. The leaders of these various groups unified their efforts, and, as a result, a steering committee of personnel administrators from various parts of the country as well as local and regional personnel associations met in Cleveland on November 20-21, 1948.

ASPA was founded at this meeting. The founding members decided to appoint a temporary slate of officers and elected Smith as chairman, Hopkins as secretary and Harry H. Willett as treasurer. The group also established six committees with responsibilities for budget and finance, conference, constitution and bylaws, membership, nominating, and publications.

The founders of ASPA agreed to meet again in Chicago for another organizational meeting in February 1949, and they also planned for the first annual membership meeting in June 1949. In addition, 21 founding members devised a temporary framework for the new society to "work out all details vital to the sound birth of a new organization," according to ASPA historian W.H. Miller in his 1977 account. Miller notes that "many of these leaders were former disillusioned members of the National Association of Personnel Directors, and since all of them were well aware of NAPD's weaknesses, they exercised extreme caution to build this framework in as democratic and as open and above board way as possible. The die was cast." (Miller, 1977)

According to Walter V. Ronner, one of the founding members of ASPA, personnel was a displaced profession at the time. He said that the "personnel man" was left out of the discussions surrounding the Wagner and Taft-Hartley Acts. Other constituents were invited by Congress to have their say, even those minimally affected, yet "no one on the firing line of management—the personnel director—was consulted."

Ronner believed that personnel directors were ignored because no national association representing personnel professionals existed. "Personnel or industrial relations has had a relatively brief heritage. ... There are no uniform standards for the profession in minds of top management, many of whom still look upon this phase of management as a stylish nuisance," Ronner said. "Nevertheless, the evolution of a national association of personnel administrators was an historical inevitability. Any profession, as it acts to reach maturity, develops definite standards, ethics and requirements. ... Therefore, we have every reason to expect that we shall soon qualify as an organized body for admission to the citizenship of industrial society."

ASPA's founders wanted the Society to offer members a clearinghouse for everything new in the personnel field. They also wanted to develop a sound code of ethics and viable qualifications for personnel administrators because they believed that a national society was the only way to weed out incompetent individuals in personnel, a major area of concern at the time. In ASPA's first brochure in December 1948, the stated purposes of the Society were:

- To constantly promote and elevate standards and performance of every phase of personnel administration, whether industrial relations, labor relations, employer-employee relations, human relations or any other name for the broad, overall functioning comprising the administration of manpower contacts and controls.

- To provide an ethical, central, national clearinghouse of authoritative data and information, and to disseminate and achieve widespread usage of better methods, more effective and more harmonious cooperation between management and labor.

- To gain recognition of and acceptance for the qualifications requisite to the adequate concept of personnel administration as one of the five basal branches of all management, equal to, and often more important than, any of the others.

- To always serve, no matter what the need, in a spirit and according to a code of ethics, never admitting of anything less than the utmost effort, knowledge and sincerity of purpose.

As the meeting ended on November 21, Ronner became the first person to apply for membership.

The NAPD's collapse provided valuable lessons about making ASPA a stronger, more enduring organization. The founders of ASPA had great expectations of this new Society, but they understood that their goals could be achieved only in the long run. They did not intend, as one founder put it, to "completely revolutionize the personnel field overnight."

With the Society's revenue limited to the $25 fees charged to each of the founding members, it was going to be difficult to do much more than concentrate on building the membership during the first years. By strictly adhering to the Society's bylaws, the founders hoped to build a powerful, influential group within five or 10 years—a group that management, labor and legislators would listen to with respect. This particular goal was so important that many founding members gave freely of their time and money to get the Society up and running.

"We all knew that we didn't want to go down that NAPD road again," said Smith. "So we looked to the more successful organizations and tried to pattern ourselves after them."

The original plans for the Society were modest and included an annual convention and four Board meetings each year. The founders also hoped to publish a periodic newsletter and to get the clearinghouse idea under way. Future plans were to produce several publications, sponsor timely conferences in conjunction with local personnel groups, establish an information bureau for members, conduct research and provide a speakers' service for any group interested in the personnel field. (Miller, 1977)

ASPA SNAPSHOT

❖ Founding members write and adopt bylaws and a code of ethics.

❖ Articles of incorporation are filed on May 8 in Cuyahoga County (Cleveland), Ohio.

❖ An ASPA office is established in Cleveland.

❖ The first Annual Conference is held June 2–3 in Cleveland.

❖ Conference attendance: 67.

❖ Conference surplus: $72.86.

❖ Membership fee: $25.

❖ Membership: 92.

❖ Female members: 6.

An ASPA office is established in Cleveland.

1949 WORLD EVENTS

- North Atlantic Treaty Organization (NATO) is formed.

- Communist forces gain power in China.

- The Soviet Union detonates its first atomic bomb.

- Nearly 500,000 steelworkers strike.

- Americans buy 100,000 television sets a week.

- Silly Putty is introduced.

- Popular movies: *The Third Man, All the King's Men.*

- Popular songs: *So in Love, Riders in the Sky, Diamonds are a Girl's Best Friend.*

- Popular TV shows: *Texaco Star Theater, Candid Camera, Kukla, Fran and Ollie.*

- Popular books: *The Egyptian,* Mika Waltari; *The Big Fisherman,* Lloyd Douglas; *Dinner at Antoine's,* Frances Parkinson Keyes.

- Average annual U.S. family income: $3,100.

By the spring of 1949, ASPA volunteers had written bylaws and a code of ethics. On May 8, articles of incorporation were filed. They were signed on June 3, 1949, during the Annual Conference, with the incorporators listed as Joseph P. Bell, John McBride and Henry J. Post.

Walter Mason was elected president of the Society, and Leonard Smith, SPHR, was elected vice president. Mary Hopkins, SPHR, served as secretary, and Harry Willett as treasurer. Nine other men were elected to complete the first ASPA Board of Directors. In addition, 14 committees were established to help run the new Society. These committees included auditing, code of ethics, conference, constitution and bylaws, executive, finance, labor relations, long-range planning, membership promotion, membership standards, nominating, publications, public relations, and research.

In August 1949, *American Business* ran an article by Walter B. Lovelace titled "New National Personnel Group Launched in Democratic Atmosphere Has Broad Aim." Lovelace wrote, "Whether or not you believe that industrial relations is a profession, we think you will be interested in ... a new national society, the American Society for Personnel Administration. The founders are hard-headed, practical personnel executives who sincerely want to raise the standards of personnel practice; weed out the imposters; have a say in important legislative matters which affect their work, and establish a clearinghouse for personnel methods and ideas."

As ASPA volunteers on the committees were building the Society's foundation, Board members were discussing the profession's need for a voice on important issues of the day. They reached out to others, and, in turn, influential leaders started reaching out to ASPA. Early in ASPA's history, Sen. Robert Taft, one of the authors of the Taft-Hartley Act, contacted ASPA President Walter Mason and asked that an ASPA representative attend hearings on the legislation. In September 1949, the Board formed a Legislative Committee to work with the Research Committee to study and make recommendations on ASPA's legislative policy.

Poodle skirts, tract homes, a national highway system and rock 'n' roll. For many, the 1950s was a time to recuperate from the effects of the Depression and World War II; to move their families to a nice, modest home in the suburbs; and to travel into the city for work on a newly built highway that cut commuting time in half. By the end of the decade, however, racial tensions in the U.S. and the Cold War would build to the boiling point.

ASPA SNAPSHOT

- The first issue of *Personnel News* is published.
- The second Annual Conference is held in Detroit.
- Conference revenue: $725.66.
- Membership fee: $25.
- Membership: 145.
- Committees: 20.

1950 WORLD EVENTS

- Communist China occupies Tibet.
- Sen. Joseph McCarthy warns of communist infiltration of the State Department.
- Congress passes laws restricting communists and communist parties in the U.S.
- Accused communist spy Alger Hiss is convicted of perjury.
- 14 million television sets are sold in the U.S., increasing the number in service tenfold.
- Popular movies: *Sunset Boulevard, All About Eve*.
- Popular songs: *A Bushel and a Peck, Good Night Irene, Mona Lisa, C'est Si Bon*.
- Popular TV shows: *Arthur Godfrey and His Friends, Your Show of Shows, Your Hit Parade*.
- Popular books: *The Martian Chronicles*, Ray Bradbury; *Across the River and Into the Trees*, Ernest Hemingway; *Darkness at Noon*, Sidney Kingsley.
- Average annual U.S. family income: $3,300.

By 1950, membership in ASPA had grown to 130. In April, ASPA published its first issue of *Personnel News*. Because the Society was still an entirely volunteer-driven organization, Walter Mason and Henry Willett served as co-editors of the new publication.

In June, ASPA held its second Annual Conference in Detroit. During the meeting, Joseph Bell was elected president, but he resigned after serving for only a few months. In October, the Board asked Mason to complete the term. Surplus for the conference that year was $725.66.

ASPA historian W.H. Miller notes that 1950 was, at least in terms of membership, a challenging time for the Society. When the Board met in February, the Society had only 96 members in good standing—just four more than the original founding membership. The Board reacted by changing the dues and membership structure, effective for 1951. "Certified professional members" were charged $25, "regular member"

ASPA SNAPSHOT

- The third Annual Conference is held in New York City.
- Conference attendance: 92.
- Conference deficit: $359.03.
- Membership fees: certified professional member, $25; regular member, $10; associate member, $10; and student member, $5.
- Membership: 217.
- Committees: 24.
- Board members: 23.
- Reserves: $7,851.46.

dues were set at $10, "associate member" dues were $10, and "student member" dues were $5. By the end of the fiscal year, membership had increased to 145.

1951 WORLD EVENTS

- North Korean forces cross the 38th parallel. Truce negotiations fail.
- Congress approves the 22nd Amendment, limiting the president to two terms in office.
- Businessman J.S. Coxey leads an unemployment protest in Washington, D.C.
- Color television is introduced. The first color broadcast is transmitted from CBS in New York City.
- In response to the growing popularity of television, movie theaters experiment with a variety of attractions, including wide-screen projection and 3-D effects.
- Popular movies: *The African Queen*, *An American in Paris*, *A Streetcar Named Desire*.
- Popular songs: *Hello Young Lovers*, *Getting to Know You*, *Cry*, *Kisses Sweeter than Wine*.
- Popular TV shows: *I Love Lucy*, *The Adventures of Ellery Queen*, *What's My Line?*
- Popular books: *A Man Called Peter*, Catherine Marshall; *Lie Down in Darkness*, William Styron; *Desirée*, Annemarie Selinko; *From Here to Eternity*, James Jones; *The Caine Mutiny*, Herman Wouk; *The Catcher in the Rye*, J.D. Salinger.
- Average annual U.S. family income: $3,700.

Leonard Smith, who had played an integral role in founding ASPA, was elected president in 1951. Ninety-two people attended the third Annual Conference in New York City. Unfortunately, the conference resulted in a deficit of $359.03.

The Society's cash reserves, however, were $7,851.46.

Membership was still rocky. At one point in the year, the number of members had dropped to 138, causing the Membership Committee to ramp up recruiting efforts. They succeeded. By the close of 1951, membership hit 217.

The November/December issue of *ASPA News* urged readers to send ASPA the names of local personnel groups because ASPA was planning an aggressive membership drive. The plan was to have ASPA volunteers speak at local group meetings to discuss the benefits of ASPA membership. At the time of publication, ASPA committee members had already contacted 200 of the groups and invited them to affiliate with the Society.

That same edition of *ASPA News* announced the formation of an employment clearinghouse, which listed two open job positions. The first was for a personnel assistant in Michigan, and the second was for a director of personnel in western Pennsylvania. The position in Michigan called "for a young man with some experience to be trained to take over the direction of the personnel department." The Pennsylvania position was for an "experienced top man in a multi-plant organization."

The Society was successfully operating under a totally volunteer structure. By the end of the year, the Board was expanded to include a first vice president and a second vice president, increasing the Board to 23 members. In addition, the Board added six new committees (chapter affiliation, awards and contests, membership services, professional standards, regional conferences, and regional planning). Two committees—executive operating and membership classification—were discontinued. Still, there were 24 committees functioning that year.

Employees commuting to work via ferry.

ASPA SNAPSHOT

Leonard Smith, who had played an integral role in founding ASPA, was elected president in 1951. Ninety-two people attended the third Annual Conference in New York City. Unfortunately, the conference resulted in a deficit of $359.03. The Society's cash reserves, however, were $7,851.46.

1952 WORLD EVENTS

- Dwight Eisenhower is elected president.

- The Korean Conflict continues as truce attempts fail.

- The U.S. detonates the world's first thermonuclear weapon.

- Britain develops the atomic bomb.

- Dr. Jonas Salk develops the polio vaccine.

- Microwave ovens are made available for domestic use. The first models are the size of refrigerators and cost more than $1,200.

- Popular movies: *Limelight, High Noon, The Greatest Show on Earth*.

- Popular songs: *It Takes Two to Tango, Your Cheatin' Heart, Wheel of Fortune*.

- Popular TV shows: *The Jackie Gleason Show, I Love Lucy, Dinah Shore*.

- Popular books: *The Old Man and the Sea*, Ernest Hemingway; *East of Eden*, John Steinbeck; *The Grass Harp*, Truman Capote; *The Power of Positive Thinking*, Norman Vincent Peale.

- Average annual U.S. family income: $3,900.

Once ASPA was on its feet and growing, it needed a place to call home. In 1952, the Board established an office at Marquette University in Milwaukee, where then ASPA President Russell Moberly, SPHR, offered office space and clerical help.

According to Leonard Smith, housing an association within the academic community was not unusual at the time. "Actually, it was quite common then to have an academic administer an association," said Smith. "Universities considered it part of the professor's professional development. They were quite generous with their support, and we were glad to have it."

The Board established 15 new committees and discontinued two, raising the total to 37 volunteer committees.

In 1952, ASPA created an affiliate system for regional personnel groups. Several strong groups were already in existence, such as the Personnel and Industrial Relations Association in Los Angeles, the New York Personnel Management Association and the Pacific Northwest Personnel Management Association. ASPA leaders wanted the Society to be national in focus but also wanted it to be relevant to such local groups.

The first group to affiliate with ASPA was the Personnel Management Association of San Diego. However, this first affiliate program did not require individual membership in the Society and was discontinued a year later in favor of the existing chapter system in which individual membership is required.

ASPA's fourth Annual Conference was held in Milwaukee, in November—the first conference to be held in the fall. Conference attendance soared from 92 in 1951 to 431 in 1952. For the first time, the conference surplus exceeded $1,000, totaling $1,139.98. In his history of ASPA, Miller notes that a "ladies' program" was held at this conference for the first time. It was so successful that the program became a feature at a number of subsequent conferences.

That year, ASPA's budget was set at $4,292.50. The Board approved changing the fiscal year to coincide with the calendar year, a change that would take effect in 1954. It turned out to be a challenging year financially for the young Society. Expenses exceeded income by more than $4,000, leaving a little more than $2,000 in reserves.

ASPA SNAPSHOT

❖ ASPA establishes its first office at Marquette University in Milwaukee.

❖ ASPA co-sponsors a personnel institute with Fairleigh Dickinson College in Rutherford, N.J.

❖ The Personnel Management Association of San Diego becomes ASPA's first affiliate.

❖ The fourth Annual Conference is held in November in Milwaukee.

❖ Conference attendance: 431.

❖ Conference surplus: $1,139.98.

❖ Membership: 230.

❖ Committees: 37.

❖ Annual budget: $4,292.50.

❖ Reserves: $2,009.82.

1953 WORLD EVENTS

- The U.S. Department of Health, Education and Welfare (now Health and Human Services) is created.

- The Soviet Union detonates its first thermonuclear bomb.

- U.S. Air Force test pilot Chuck Yeager sets a speed record in an X-1 rocket plane.

- An expedition led by Sir Edmund Hillary is the first to reach the summit of Mount Everest.

- Popular movies: *Roman Holiday, From Here to Eternity, The Robe.*

- Popular songs: *Doggie in the Window, I Believe, I Love Paris.*

- Popular TV shows: *Twenty Questions, Red Skelton Show, Make Room for Daddy.*

- Popular books: *Casino Royale*, Ian Fleming; *Battle Cry*, Leon Uris.

- Average annual U.S. family income: $4,200.

ASPA's leaders continued to seek ways to establish the Society as a national professional association. In February 1953, the Board of Directors, under the direction of ASPA President Russell Moberly, divided the country into six regions—each one headed by a regional director, with one to six district representatives to handle the smaller business and industrial areas within each region. The purpose of this move was for all administrative policies and procedures of the Society and the membership to be handled through this new administrative organization.

In 1953, the Society's first library was established at Marquette University in Milwaukee through member donations. Membership blossomed. By the end of 1953, there were 467 ASPA members, more than double the previous year's membership.

The fifth ASPA Annual Conference did not fare as well. Held in November in St. Louis, there were only 252 attendees, nearly 200 less than the previous conference. The conference ran a deficit of $1,394.82. In spite of the setback, the Society still ended the year with "slightly more surplus than the previous term." (Miller, 1977)

1954 WORLD EVENTS

- The Supreme Court rules that race-based segregation in schools is unconstitutional.

- Sen. Joseph McCarthy conducts nationally televised inquiries into communist infiltration of the Army; his activities are condemned by the Senate.

- The phrase "under God" is added to the Pledge of Allegiance.

- *The Practice of Management* by Peter Drucker is published.

- Popular movies: *On the Waterfront, Rear Window, The Seven Samurai.*

- Popular songs: *Three Coins in a Fountain, Mister Sandman, Young at Heart.*

- Popular TV shows: *The Jack Benny Program, The Adventures of Rin Tin Tin, The George Gobel Show, Disneyland.*

- Popular books: *A Stillness at Appomattox*, Bruce Catton; *The Lord of the Rings*, J.R.R. Tolkien; *Lord of the Flies*, William Golding.

- Average annual U.S. family income: $4,200.

In 1954, Peter Drucker's *The Practice of Management* was published and the term "human resources" was born. In the book, Drucker presented three broad managerial functions: managing the business, managing other managers, and managing workers and work. It was in the discussion of the management of workers and work that Drucker introduced

ASPA SNAPSHOT

- The Board is expanded from 23 members to 28 to accommodate new regional vice president positions. The fiscal year is now based on a calendar year.

- The annual membership meeting is discontinued. Voting is now conducted by mail, and a business meeting is held at the Annual Conference.

- One new committee, the International Relations Committee, is established. Eight existing committees are discontinued. Total committees: 30.

- The *Journal for Personnel Administration*, edited by Sterling Schoen, is first published.

- The certified professional member membership class is eliminated. Regular and associate member dues are raised to $18; chapters receive a $3 refund for regular and associate members in the chapter.

- The Board approves hiring an executive director.

- The Annual Conference is held in Cincinnati.

- Conference attendance: 290.

- Conference surplus: $2,436.49.

- Membership: 545.

- Annual budget: $10,500.

- Reserves: $5,403.51.

the concept of the worker as "the human resource." He said that "the human resource" possesses a quality that is not present in other resources: "the ability to coordinate, to integrate, to judge and to imagine." He added, "The human being ... has absolute control over whether he works at all."

Drucker saw three basic flaws in the personnel management discipline of the 1950s. He stated that the personnel management field operated under the assumptions that: 1) people did not want to work; 2) the management of work and the worker was a specialist's job rather than a key part of any manager's job; and 3) management had the tendency to be a "firefighting" and "troubleshooting" activity, rather than one focusing on the positive and on building harmony.

By the end of 1954, ASPA had 545 members, an increase of 78 for the year. In addition, three more chapters had joined the Society for a total of five. The Society was becoming more firmly established, and with the additional members and chapters, administrative details were steadily mounting (Miller, 1977). In September, the Board approved the addition of a paid executive director, to be employed and housed at Marquette University in Milwaukee at a salary not to exceed $9,000, effective January 1, 1955. The location was later changed to East Lansing, Mich., with a starting date of January 1, 1956. In the minutes of the meeting, the Board said it thought it probable that a "good man" could be found for the job.

The Board established one new committee, the International Relations Committee, and discontinued eight committees—conference policy, functional, Canadian membership, membership services, membership standards, regional conferences, steering and top management relations. There were now 30 working committees reporting to the Board.

The Society added to its publications when it published the first volume of the *Journal for Personnel Administration* in October. The journal featured the proceedings of the 1953 Annual Conference and little else.

Annual dues were raised to $18 for regular members and associate members, and the certified professional member membership class was eliminated because the Board could not agree to standards for that category. Chapters would receive $3 back for each regular and associate member in the chapter.

The sixth Annual Conference was held that year in Cincinnati. There were 290 paid attendees and a $2,436.49 surplus. The budget for the year was set at $10,500—representing the first time the annual budget exceeded $10,000. Revenue was $14,445.49; expenses were $12,377.30. The Society now had $5,403.51 in reserves and appeared to be growing stronger.

1955 WORLD EVENTS

- Dr. Martin Luther King Jr. leads the bus boycott in Montgomery, Ala.
- The Interstate Commerce Commission orders all U.S. interstate trains and buses to end segregation.
- The American Federation of Labor (AFL) and the Congress of Industrial Organizations (CIO) merge.
- Rudolph Flesch writes *Why Johnny Can't Read*, a stinging criticism of U.S. education.
- Popular movies: *Marty, The Seven Year Itch, Smiles of a Summer Night.*

According to the 1954 bylaws, the purpose of the Society was "to advance and develop ethics, methods and research toward higher standards of performance in personnel administration." ASPA's tagline: To Advance and Develop Personnel Ethics, Methods and Research.

- Popular songs: *Rock Around the Clock, The Yellow Rose of Texas, Davy Crockett.*
- Popular TV shows: *The Lawrence Welk Show, The Honeymooners, Gunsmoke, Lassie.*
- Popular books: *The Man in the Gray Flannel Suit,* Sloan Wilson; *Lolita,* Vladimir Nabokov; *Witness for the Prosecution,* Agatha Christie.
- Average annual U.S. family income: $4,400.

The Board continued to grapple with membership classes and the dues structure. The bylaws were amended to allow for corporate memberships. In September, the Board approved an "affiliate" class of membership, with annual dues of $5, and a "company" class of membership, with annual dues of $50 for the first three members and $50 more for each additional group of four members or less. ASPA historian W.H. Miller notes that the affiliate membership class was established to "speed up the acquisition of new chapters ... and to increase individual ASPA membership within the [existing] chapters." (Miller, 1977)

The second and last issue of the *Journal for Personnel Administration* was published in May and covered the 1954 conference proceedings. The proceedings for future conferences were intended to be reported in *Personnel News.*

That same year, the ASPA Board began to discuss the possibility of creating an ASPA Foundation. A committee was appointed to explore the plan, and later in the year, the Board agreed to appoint a committee to draw up proposals for the structure and organization of a foundation.

Another committee, the Trade Group Committee, was formed, and four committees were discontinued. The discontinued committees were labor relations, man-of-the-year (no awards were made), regional planning and research projects. After the changes, 28 volunteer committees reported to the Board.

The Annual Conference was again held in November, this time in Chicago. There were 240 attendees and a conference surplus of $5,542.74, attributed in large part to revenue from exhibitors.

This is the first year Miller mentions a pre-conference cocktail party for "ASPA officers, directors, conference committee members, and their ladies." The cocktail party was sponsored by Pepsi-Cola Company. Miller notes that "[t]his was a 'gratis' party held for the first time and through the generosity of the Pepsi-Cola Company, and this became a regular, looked forward to, pre-conference event which has been held for ASPA every year since." (Miller, 1977)

This is also the first year that the Society named an "official jeweler." The Gordon B. Miller Company was selected and remained the Society's official jeweler through 1960. The company provided emblem jewelry and plaques that Society members and chapters could purchase.

During the November Board meeting, the Board approved the employment of Paul L. Moore to become the Society's first executive director. The budget was set for $10,800. Actual revenue was $13,836.86, and expenditures were $12,620.44. The Society had reserves of $6,619.93. For the first time in several years, membership decreased—from 545 in 1954 to 503 in 1955.

ASPA SNAPSHOT

- ✧ Corporate memberships are allowed.

- ✧ The *Journal for Personnel Administration* is discontinued after its second publication.

- ✧ The Board approves Paul L. Moore to become ASPA's first executive director.

- ✧ Conference attendance: 240.

- ◊ Conference surplus: $5,542.74.

- ✧ Membership: 503.

- ✧ Committees: 28.

- ✧ Reserves: $6,619.93.

The *Journal for Personnel Administration*, edited by Sterling Schoen, is first published.

1956 WORLD EVENTS

- ▪ President Eisenhower is re-elected.

- ▪ Congress approves the Highway Act, authorizing the construction of the U.S. interstate highway system. This Act fuels the suburbanization of America.

- ▪ The first transatlantic telephone cable goes into operation.

- ▪ Elvis Presley becomes a national phenomenon.

- ▪ The minimum wage is $1 per hour.

- ▪ Popular movies: *The Ten Commandments, Lust for Life, Around the World in 80 Days.*

- ▪ Popular songs: *Don't Be Cruel, Blue Suede Shoes, Hound Dog, I Could Have Danced All Night.*

- ▪ Popular TV shows: *The Danny Thomas Show, The Perry Como Show, Ed Sullivan Show.*

- ▪ Popular books: *Peyton Place*, Grace Metalious; *Profiles in Courage*, John F. Kennedy; *The Last Hurrah*, Edwin O'Connor.

- ▪ Average annual U.S. family income: $4,800.

In 1956, the Board recognized that the Society should have a voice in legislative matters and established a new Labor Relations Committee by combining two committees (the National Legislative Reporting Committee and the existing Labor Relations Committee). It was agreed that the committee would confine itself to four categories of work: 1) negotiation, 2) mediation and conciliation, 3) grievances and arbitration, and 4) legislation.

That year, Congress was considering legislation to address such issues as protecting and conserving labor health and welfare funds and balancing the legal responsibility of unions and employers under the Taft-Hartley Act. Some of the key issues included allowing secret ballots for initiating strikes and invalidating contracts that included unfair labor practices. The legislation was designed to eliminate loopholes in the Taft-Hartley Act and to define the rights of and create protections for the public whenever labor disputes threatened the health and safety of the general populace.

The congressional interest in workplace issues created a dilemma for the Society, and the members discussed how they should respond. During one meeting, a Board member commented that "ASPA cannot expect to be effective in personal representation before Congress. We can, however, wield a heavy influence in support of such organizations as the Chamber of Commerce of the United States, the National Association of Manufacturers, and the almost innumerable trade associations such as NRDGA, Retail Federation of America, etc." The Board later agreed that the Society "should take no position [on legislative matters] other than to maintain a consistently professional approach except as approved specifically by the Board of Directors."

While Congress examined the effect of organized labor on the workforce, the members of ASPA took note of another evolving trend. In November, in recognition of the increasing role of women in the field and their involvement in the Society, the Board of Directors approved the formation of a new committee, the Women in Personnel Committee.

The face of ASPA's workforce was changing, too. At the beginning of the year, Paul Moore, assistant to the director of the continuing education service at Michigan State University in East Lansing, Mich., was appointed ASPA's first executive vice president and the Society's first paid staff member. Moore would hold that position until 1965. He had arranged for office space and clerical support at Michigan State. While Moore still remained an employee at Michigan State, he also received a salary from ASPA. The

ASPA SNAPSHOT

university was generous enough to pay Moore's assistant, who performed clerical work for the Society.

The Board of Directors had debated over the years whether to continue publishing both *Personnel News* and the *Journal for Personnel Administration.* In the end, the Board decided to create a single publication called *The Personnel Administrator.* The new magazine would be longer than the existing *Personnel News*, with more space devoted to articles of a professional nature and a portion of the magazine devoted to news items about Society activities and the activities of individual members.

In April 1956, the first issue of *The Personnel Administrator* rolled off the presses. Articles that year included "The Guaranteed Annual Wage," "Successful Attack on Absenteeism" and "How Insurance Companies Feel About Employing the Handicapped in Industry." The magazine's name would stick for 34 years until it was renamed *HR Magazine* in January 1990.

By the end of 1956, ASPA had 685 members. The eighth Annual Conference was held in April in Kansas City, Mo., with 307 attendees. The conference surplus was $2,881.07. Five new chapters were added. Finally, the ASPA Foundation was founded in October, with Leonard Brice, SPHR, serving as its first president.

1957 WORLD EVENTS

- The Space Race begins in October when the Soviet Union launches Sputnik I. A month later, Sputnik II is launched and carries a dog into orbit.

- Federal troops are ordered to enforce the integration of schools in Little Rock, Ark.

- The Civil Rights Act of 1957 is passed.

- The Southern Christian Leadership Conference is founded by Dr. Martin Luther King Jr.

- The Teamsters union is expelled from the AFL-CIO for failing to deal with organized crime.

- The term "beatnik" becomes popular in describing the new and emerging counterculture movement known as the "beat generation."

- Popular movies: *The Bridge on the River Kwai, The Prince and the Showgirl, Twelve Angry Men.*

- Popular songs: *Wake Up Little Susie, That'll Be the Day, Jailhouse Rock.*

- Popular TV shows: *Father Knows Best, American Bandstand, Leave it to Beaver, The Nat King Cole Show.*

- Popular books: *On the Road,* Jack Kerouac; *Atlas Shrugged,* Ayn Rand; *The Cat in the Hat,* Dr. Seuss.

- Average annual U.S. family income: $5,000.

If your recollection of the 1950s is based on the 1970s TV sitcom *Happy Days*, you may not realize that the 1950s were, in fact, pretty difficult times. The decade started with the U.S. entering into the Korean Conflict. Communism was the enemy, and anyone thought to be associated with it was un-American. The civil rights movement gained momentum, causing tension and, unfortunately, violence in the United States. The events of the 1950s—a decade usually associated with conservatism—fed into the social movement of the 1960s.

ASPA SNAPSHOT

- The Milwaukee office is closed when the office in East Lansing, Mich., opens. The East Lansing office is staffed by Paul Moore and one part-time employee.

- A request is made to the U.S. Patent Office to trademark ASPA.

- One new committee, the Past Presidents Committee, is formed, and the Conference Site Committee is discontinued. Total committees: 27.

- John Boyer becomes editor of *The Personnel Administrator.*

- An increase in membership dues (effective for 1959) is approved. Regular and associate membership dues are raised to $25, and student membership dues are raised to $10. Company membership is increased to $100.

- Conference attendance: 236.

- Conference surplus: $2,253.22.

- Membership: 1,212.

- Reserves: $1,540.95.

1957 was particularly eventful: The Southern Christian Leadership Conference headed by Dr. Martin Luther King Jr. was formed; President Eisenhower sent federal troops to Little Rock, Ark., to ensure that African-American students could enroll at Central High School after they were blocked from entering on order of Governor Orval Faubus; and the Civil Rights Act of 1957 was passed, establishing a Civil Rights Commission and a civil rights division in the Department of Justice to prevent interference with the right to vote.

ASPA was experiencing its own changes, but not as radical. The first ASPA office in Milwaukee was closed when the office opened in East Lansing, Mich., and Paul Moore came aboard as the Society's first executive vice president.

Membership in the organization jumped sharply that year—from 685 to 1,212, blowing the targeted (and challenging) goal of 1,000 out of the water.

The changes, however, came at a cost. The 1957 budget was set at $18,550. Actual revenue came in at $16,662.15, and expenses were $15,475.97, for a surplus of only $1,186.18, bringing the total reserves to $1,540.95. ASPA historian W.H. Miller notes in his history of the Society that "This … was the turning point and the last extremely low balance of society surplus funds. ASPA's 'childhood' status was at an end."

The first article that focused solely on the future of the HR profession ran in an issue of *The Personnel Administrator* that year. Professor Peter Calhoon from the University of North Carolina wrote in his article "The Eventuation of Personnel Administration" that the "personnel administrator is a relatively new member of management and his responsibilities have grown in part due to changing concepts, which in turn have been influenced by factors affecting business."

Growing organization size, unionization, increasing government regulations and economic stability were feeding business and, in turn, the personnel management profession. Calhoon warned "personnel men," however, that they were not yet ready to lead their organizations into the future. He felt that line management was distrusting of personnel and frequently engaged in turf wars to have more control over employment decisions. He also felt that there were still too many "weak personnel men" in the field and that the overall professionalism needed to be raised and erroneous assumptions about the field needed to be addressed.

Calhoon wrote that the erroneous assumptions about the HR profession were that:

- It required no special training; anyone could do it.

- It was basically a clerical, recordkeeping job.

- It was a consulting position that should be used when called on by line managers (and that should stay quiet when not called on).

- Its main function was to develop policies and procedures for line managers' use. After the policies and procedures were developed, it should stay out of the way of the line managers.

- Personnel work covered the individual relationships in the workplace and was subordinate to the more important functions of labor relations, public relations and human relations.

ASPA SNAPSHOT

- The first lifetime membership is presented to Russell Moberly during the Annual Conference.
- The Annual Conference is held in Philadelphia.
- Conference attendance: 271.
- Conference surplus: $3,642.81.
- Membership: 1,490.
- Chapters: 19.
- Committees: 30.
- Revenue: $31,173.58.
- Reserves: $7,046.06.

1958 WORLD EVENTS

- The U.S. launches its first satellite, Explorer I; the National Aeronautics and Space Administration (NASA) is formed.
- National Airlines launches the first domestic jet-airline passenger service with a flight between New York City and Miami.
- Vice President Richard Nixon's goodwill tour of South America sparks protests and rioting.
- An economic slowdown in the U.S. causes a sharp rise in unemployment.
- Union membership totals almost 39 percent of the workforce.
- Hula hoops are a national craze.
- Popular movies: *Gigi, Cat on a Hot Tin Roof, Me and the Colonel.*
- Popular songs: *Catch a Falling Star, Chipmunk Song, Volare.*
- Popular TV shows: *Wagon Train, To Tell the Truth, The Rifleman.*
- Popular books: *A Raisin in the Sun,* Lorraine Hansberry; *Exodus,* Leon Uris; *Dr. Zhivago,* Boris Pasternak.
- Average annual U.S. family income: $5,100.

1958 was a good year for ASPA. The conference was a success, and membership hit an all-time high. The budget was set at a little more than $16,000 that year, but because dues income came in December for 1959 membership, actual income for the year was more than $31,000. The Society's cash reserves were at their highest point since 1951.

Charles Davis became editor of *The Personnel Administrator,* effective with the February edition. The Society also appointed its first advertising manager for the magazine, Melvin Byers. The February issue of the magazine featured the article "What Plant Managers Expect of Personnel Managers." Another issue tackled in the magazine that year was the effect of the baby-boom generation on the workplace, in which the article's author, Ewan Clague,

commissioner of labor statistics at the U.S. Department of Labor, examined the challenges the post-war population boom would pose. "Employers, therefore, must recognize that during the coming years, they will be facing a shortage of prime workers, grouped with a steady increase in older workers, and a flood of young workers needing to be trained," Clague wrote.

This was the year the magazine first began accepting advertising, a benefit of increased circulation. The June 1958 issue ran the first four paid advertisements, including ads for Pepsi—"A Pepsi break for efficiency's sake"—Owens-Illinois Glassware and an ASPA Christmas tote bag filled with 10 children's toys.

Two more chapters affiliated with ASPA that year, for a total of 19 chapters. Although chapter affiliation remained slow, ASPA leaders were confident that the number of affiliating chapters would pick up in coming years.

1959 WORLD EVENTS

- Alaska and Hawaii become the 49th and 50th states.
- Fidel Castro becomes premier of Cuba.
- The Landrum-Griffin Act, also known as the Labor-Management Reporting and Disclosure Act, is passed to control unfair union practices. It prohibits secondary boycotts, provides certain protections for the rights of union members, and requires the filing of financial reports by both unions and employers.
- A small plane carrying Buddy Holly, Ritchie Valens and the Big Bopper crashes during an Iowa snowstorm, killing everyone onboard. The tragedy is later immortalized as "The Day the Music Died" in Don McLean's song *American Pie.*
- The Frisbee makes its debut.
- The *Twilight Zone* premieres.

ASPA SNAPSHOT

- The dues increase approved in 1957 goes into effect.
- There are now one part-time and two full-time employees working in the East Lansing, Mich., office.
- W.H. Miller is appointed as ASPA historian, a position he maintains until 1977.
- 13 regular chapters and two student chapters affiliate. ASPA now has chapters in 15 states and the District of Columbia.
- The Annual Conference is held in Milwaukee.
- Conference attendance: 390.
- Conference surplus: $5,291.08.
- Membership: 1,757.
- Committees: 35.
- Reserves: $17,755.14.

- Scandal rocks the TV quiz show *$64,000 Question* when a contestant admits his winning performances were rigged.
- Popular movies: *Suddenly, Last Summer; Ben-Hur; Anatomy of a Murder.*
- Popular songs: *Mack the Knife, High Hopes, Personality.*
- Popular TV shows: *Maverick, Rawhide, Dennis the Menace.*
- Popular books: *Goodbye, Columbus*, Philip Roth; *Goldfinger*, Ian Fleming; *The Miracle Worker*, William Gibson.
- Average annual U.S. family income: $5,400.

The dues increase did not seem to cause any backlash; by the end of 1959, ASPA had nearly 1,800 members. The Annual Conference was growing, both in terms of the number of attendees and the money it contributed to the Society. The number of chapters affiliating with the Society also increased significantly.

The growing number of women in the workplace was grabbing more attention, and the October cover story for *The Personnel Administrator*, "Womanpower—A National Asset" by Alice K. Leopold, assistant to the U.S. secretary of labor, clearly reflected this trend.

In the March issue of the magazine, Paul Moore wrote that many of the objectives commonly subscribed to by personnel people—professionalism of those engaged in personnel, upgrading the competence of people engaged in personnel work, adherence to an established code of ethics, and a need for greater appreciation of the personnel function by people in general and management in particular—could not be achieved without collective effort, specifically through a strong organization like ASPA.

Competitors at the time included the Society for Personnel Administration, the Industrial Relations Research Association, and the American Academy of Personnel Executives. The bulk of ASPA's membership was made up of industrial and business personnel administrators. A majority carried the title of vice president, director or manager of either industrial relations or personnel. White-collar industries such as banks, insurance companies and municipalities were gaining in representation, and a substantial number of members were in government personnel work.

Benefits of Membership in ASPA in 1959

- Periodicals, including *The Personnel Administrator*.
- National conferences.
- Free use of the ASPA Personnel Library at Marquette University.
- The prestige of membership (similar to that enjoyed by the physician who belongs to the American Medical Association or the lawyer who is a member of the American Bar Association).
- Placement service for those seeking jobs or those seeking to fill positions.
- A copy of the national *Directory of Personnel Administrators*.
- Exchange of information with others in the profession.
- An opportunity to share in national policy formation.
- Service on one of the 35 active national committees if qualified and interested.
- An opportunity for acquaintance and fellowship with leading personnel administrators.
- Periodic mailings of the results of research studies and other carefully selected pieces of worthwhile information.

RECAP OF KEY EVENTS IN HUMAN RESOURCE MANAGEMENT

1947–1959

1947   The Labor Management Relations (Taft-Hartley) Act is enacted.

1948   The American Society for Personnel Administration (ASPA) is established.

1949   ASPA holds its first Annual Conference. Walter Mason becomes the first ASPA president.

1952   The Personnel Management Association of San Diego becomes ASPA's first affiliate.

1953   The Metropolitan New York Personnel Group becomes ASPA's first chapter.

1955   The AFL-CIO is established.

1956   Paul L. Moore becomes the first head of ASPA as executive vice president.

1956   *The Personnel Administrator* (now *HR Magazine*) is first published.

1959   The Labor-Management Reporting and Disclosure (Landrum-Griffin) Act is enacted.

1959   ASPA membership reaches 1,757.

chapter

1960s

three

ASPA SNAPSHOT

❖ Two delegates are appointed to represent ASPA at a White House conference on aging.

❖ ASPA establishes a publications office at Colorado State University in Fort Collins, Colo. Ray O. Davies, the Society's first honorary life member, becomes part-time editor of *The Personnel Administrator*.

❖ A full-time employee is added to the office in East Lansing, Mich., bringing the total number of employees to four (three full time and one part time).

❖ The Annual Conference is held in New York City.

❖ Conference attendance: 382.

❖ Conference surplus: $50.54.

❖ Membership: 2,029.

❖ Committees: 22.

❖ Annual budget: $42,450.

❖ Reserves: $18,167.67.

If the 1950s are remembered as a conservative decade, the 1960s are remembered for radicalism, both politically and socially. By the mid-1960s, the U.S. was embroiled in the Vietnam Conflict, and protests against the war occurred with increasing frequency. Dissatisfaction across the country with the war coincided with the civil rights demonstrations that swept across the nation. By 1972, the anti-war movement was strong, with middle-class and business professionals joining students and armed services personnel in the protests. For many, an important link was established between the war abroad and the poverty and racial divide at home.

1960 WORLD EVENTS

- John F. Kennedy is elected president.

- African-American students stage a sit-in at a lunch counter in Greensboro, N.C., to protest segregated seating. The event inspires a wave of sit-ins across the South.

- The number of television sets in the U.S. reaches 85 million—nearly one set for every two Americans.

- Popular movies: *Psycho, The Entertainer, The Apartment.*

- Popular songs: *Itsy Bitsy Teeny Weenie Yellow Polka Dot Bikini, Let's Do the Twist, Teen Angel.*

- Popular TV shows: *Perry Mason, Bonanza, My Three Sons, The Andy Griffith Show.*

- Popular books: *The Affair*, C.P. Snow; *To Kill a Mockingbird*, Harper Lee; *Rabbit, Run*, John Updike.

- Average annual U.S. family income: $5,600.

ASPA opened the decade on a strong note. Membership continued to grow, with 272 new members added in 1960 to top 2,000 for the first time. The budget was more than $42,000 that year, and despite a small surplus from conference revenues, the Society had more than $18,000 in reserves.

The East Lansing office, located on the Michigan State campus, hired another full-time employee, but the office staff were increasingly overworked. The Board approved opening a publications office in Fort Collins, Colo., on the Colorado State University campus. Ray O. Davies was appointed editor of *The Personnel Administrator*. Davies worked as a volunteer (in an unsalaried position), and the university provided office space and part-time clerical support—much like the arrangement with Michigan State University.

Astronaut Edwin E. "Buzz" Aldrin Jr. poses for a photograph beside the U.S. flag deployed on the moon during the Apollo 11 mission on July 20, 1969. Aldrin and fellow astronaut Neil Armstrong were the first men to walk on the lunar surface with temperatures ranging from 243 degrees above to 279 degrees below zero. Astronaut Michael Collins flew the command module. (AP Photo/Neil Armstrong, NASA)

U.S. businesses and workers continued to prosper, despite the 1960s being a turbulent decade. As an organization, ASPA reflected none of that turbulence.

ASPA SNAPSHOT

- ✦ The Annual Conference is held in Minneapolis.
- ✦ Conference attendance: 381.
- ✦ Conference exhibitors: 24.
- ✦ Conference surplus: $8,398.81.
- ✦ Membership: 2,394.
- ✦ Committees: 20.
- ✦ Annual budget: $40,300.
- ✦ Reserves: $20,966.32.

1961 WORLD EVENTS

- The Peace Corps is established.
- The Soviets build the Berlin Wall, dividing East and West Berlin.
- Freedom Riders travel to the Southern United States to promote integration.
- Alan Shepard becomes the first American in space.
- Popular movies: *West Side Story, The Hustler, Judgment at Nuremberg.*
- Popular songs: *Moon River, Will You Love Me Tomorrow, Blue Moon.*
- Popular TV shows: *The Rocky and Bullwinkle Show, Hazel, The Dick Van Dyke Show.*
- Popular books: *Stranger in a Strange Land*, Robert Heinlein; *Catch-22*, Joseph Heller; *The Carpetbaggers*, Harold Robbins.
- Average annual U.S. family income: $5,700.

On March 6, 1961, President Kennedy issued Executive Order 10925, creating the Committee on Equal Employment Opportunity and mandating that work projects and contracts financed with federal funds "take affirmative action" to ensure that hiring and employment practices were free of racial bias.

ASPA continued its steady growth. The Society's leaders continued to follow in the founders' footsteps, focusing on building a strong foundation to ensure that the Society was well-positioned to continue far into the future.

A 1961 issue of *The Personnel Administrator* praised the successful conference in Minneapolis, reporting that "the speakers were, without exception, authoritative and articulate. Fun highlights were the trip to the famous 'Old Log Theatre,' featuring a dinner and special show; the Annual Social Hour and Banquet at which Dr. George Heaton was the speaker; and for the ladies—Grayline sightseeing tours, a visit and luncheon at the famous Betty Crocker Kitchen, and a behind the scenes tour of 'Southdale,' the world's largest and most modern shopping center."

1962 WORLD EVENTS

- The Cuban Missile Crisis further deteriorates U.S.-Soviet relations, heightening Cold War tensions.
- John Glenn becomes the first American to orbit the earth.
- Popular movies: *Spartacus, West Side Story, The Music Man.*
- Popular songs: *Blowin' in the Wind, The Loco-Motion, Monster Mash, Big Girls Don't Cry.*
- Popular TV shows: *I've Got a Secret, The Beverly Hillbillies, The Flintstones.*
- Popular books: *Who's Afraid of Virginia Woolf?*, Edward Albee; *Travels with Charley*, John Steinbeck; *One Flew Over the Cuckoo's Nest*, Ken Kesey.
- Average annual U.S. family income: $6,000.

ASPA began playing a more prominent role in government affairs. Building on the Board's appointment in 1960 of two members to serve as delegates to a White House conference on aging, in 1962 delegates were appointed by then ASPA President Theo Mitchelson to represent the Society with the Industrial Relations Council of the National Association of Manufacturers, the Federation of Management Organizations, the Academy of Political and Social Science, and the Governor's Committee on Hiring the Handicapped.

1963 WORLD EVENTS

- President Kennedy is assassinated in Dallas. Vice President Lyndon Johnson is inaugurated president. The accused assassin, Lee Harvey Oswald, is shot and killed three days later.

ASPA SNAPSHOT

- The Annual Conference is held in Jacksonville, Fla.

- Conference attendance: 362.

- Conference surplus: $5,918.09.

- Membership: 2,892.

- Committees: 23.

- Staff: Seven (five full time and two part time).

- Annual budget: $53,500.

- Reserves: $29,142.47.

November 26, 1964, issue of *The Berea News* about ASPA selecting Berea as its new headquarters location.

- Civil rights protests continue throughout the South. Nonviolent activists are frequently met with beatings and arrests.

- 200,000 people march on Washington in support of civil rights; Dr. Martin Luther King Jr. delivers his "I Have a Dream" speech.

- Unemployment reaches 6.1 percent.

- The Equal Pay Act is enacted.

- Popular movies: *Dr. Strangelove, The Birds, Tom Jones.*

- Popular songs: *Go Away Little Girl, He's So Fine, It's My Party.*

- Popular TV shows: *My Favorite Martian, 77 Sunset Strip, McHale's Navy.*

- Popular books: *In the Clearing*, Robert Frost; *The Guns of August*, Barbara Tuchman; *The Spy Who Came in from the Cold*, John le Carré.

- Average annual U.S. family income: $6,200.

1963 was a turbulent year for Americans. President Kennedy was assassinated on November 22 in Dallas. Dr. Martin Luther King Jr. and 200,000 of his followers marched on Washington in support of civil rights, and Dr. King delivered his famous "I Have a Dream" speech from the steps of the Lincoln Memorial. Civil rights demonstrations continued throughout the South, and many nonviolent protestors were beaten and arrested.

The Feminine Mystique by Betty Friedan was published that year. The book was the outcome of a survey Friedan sent her 1942 graduating class from Smith College. Friedan and her classmates all noted a general dissatisfaction in their lives. In the book, she wrote:

"If I am right, the problem that has no name stirring in the minds of so many American women today is not a matter of loss of femininity or too much education, or the demands of domesticity. It is far more important than anyone recognizes. It is the key to these other new and old problems which have been torturing women and their husbands and children, and puzzling their doctors and educators for years. It may well be the key to our future as a nation and a culture. We can no longer ignore that voice within women that says: 'I want something more than my husband and my children and my home.' "

The feminist movement—like the civil rights movement—had begun and could not be stopped. The Equal Pay Act, passed in 1963, prohibited wage differentials based on sex for workers covered by the Fair Labor Standards Act and prohibited lowering the wages of one sex in order to prevent raising pay for the other.

The 1960s had entered its full rebellious swing.

ASPA reflects none of the 1960s turbulence. W.H. Miller's history notes that in 1963, in addition to continued growth of conference attendance, revenue and membership, ASPA established an annual research contest for members. Also that year, ASPA's first librarian, Celia Hauck, was appointed to head the Society's library at Marquette University. The number of ASPA chapters approached 60.

1964 WORLD EVENTS

- President Johnson is re-elected in a landslide over Barry Goldwater.

- Three civil rights workers are murdered in Mississippi during "Freedom Summer."

ASPA SNAPSHOT

❖ A new publication for volunteer leaders, *Leaders Forum*, is launched.

❖ The Annual Conference is held in Cleveland.

❖ Conference attendance: 300.

❖ Conference surplus: $6,503.72.

❖ Membership: 3,000.

❖ Committees: 22.

❖ Annual budget: $56,030.

❖ Reserves: $33,207.19.

ASPA promotional material from 1960.

- The 24th Amendment to the Constitution ensuring fair voting practices is ratified.

- The Civil Rights Act of 1964 is signed into law; Title VII of the Act makes it unlawful for employers to discriminate against workers based on race, sex, religion and national origin.

- Race riots begin breaking out in U.S. cities.

- Teamsters President Jimmy Hoffa is convicted of fraud, conspiracy and jury tampering.

- The Beatles become a global phenomenon.

- Popular movies: *Lord of the Flies, A Hard Day's Night, My Fair Lady*.

- Popular songs: *I Want to Hold Your Hand, Can't Buy Me Love, Oh, Pretty Woman*.

- Popular TV shows: *Gomer Pyle, U.S.M.C.; Bonanza; Bewitched*.

- Popular books: *A Moveable Feast*, Ernest Hemingway; *In His Own Write*, John Lennon.

- Average annual U.S. family income: $6,600.

As the country continued to struggle with its demons, ASPA continued to build on its solid foundation. The ASPA Board had long recognized the importance of developing future leaders in personnel administration. In 1964, the Board agreed to experiment with a pilot student chapter at Indiana University (the first two student chapters which had affiliated in 1959 had folded). Following the success of the pilot chapter, ASPA launched its student chapter program, with Indiana University and Adelphia College as the Society's first student chapters.

With its increasing success, the Society had outgrown its offices in Wisconsin, Michigan and Colorado, which had been provided to ASPA through the generous support of three universities and their faculty. With an eye toward the future, ASPA leaders hired a full-time staff person to run operations out of a single office.

It was not an easy decision. In fact, the Board had rejected the idea several times. George Trombold, SPHR, who served as chair in 1964, said that "there were quite a few Board members who were against hiring any staff person. But frankly, as volunteers, we just couldn't handle it any longer. It had gotten too big." Trombold said that some Board members still harbored painful memories of the National Association of Personnel Directors and were concerned about turning over most of the control to someone who might ultimately destroy it.

Long-time volunteer and former chair Leonard Brice, SPHR, was hired as ASPA's newest executive vice president on November 11, 1964. Sites for the new offices were narrowed to three locations based on the location of the majority of ASPA members and chapters: Chicago-Des Plaines, Berea-Cleveland and Cincinnati. The Board decided on the Berea-Cleveland area. ASPA leaders signed a lease for 600 square feet of office space at 52 East Bridge Street in Berea at a cost of $1,500 per year. By now, ASPA had more than 3,000 members, nearly 70 chapters and an annual budget of almost $65,000.

The July/August issue of *The Personnel Administrator* ran "Women at Work: One of the Most Controversial Issues of the Sixties" by Dr. Daniel Kruger. Dr. Kruger looked at the societal forces, labor demand issues and economic issues that compelled women into the workforce in the 1960s. In the article, he wrote that "our concern here is with the role of women in the labor force. We leave to others to discuss

ASPA SNAPSHOT

- Leonard Brice, SPHR, is named executive vice president, replacing a retiring Paul Moore.

- The Board approves opening a new national office in Berea, Ohio, and closing the East Lansing, Mich., office.

- Leaders Forum is discontinued; ASPA Action will be its replacement.

- The Annual Conference is held in St. Louis.

- Conference attendance: 385.

- Conference surplus: $1,642.40.

- Membership: 3,152.

- Chapters: 67.

- Committees: 22.

- Annual budget: $64,400.

- Reserves: $32.243.56.

The Board approves opening a new national office in Berea, Ohio, and closing the East Lansing, Mich., office.

the impact of working women on family life, mental health, juvenile delinquency and on society as a whole."

The Space Race heated up in the 1960s, and technology became a hot topic, not only in popular culture but in the Society's magazine as well. The first ad for a new computerized personnel information system appeared in the July/August issue. Most of the technology articles focused on the challenges posed by automation and the pitfalls of replacing workers with machinery.

1965 WORLD EVENTS

- In March, 200 Alabama state troopers clash with 525 civil rights demonstrators.

- 3,500 Marines arrive in South Vietnam in March, becoming the first American combat troops in the country. In July, President Johnson increases the number of troops in South Vietnam from 75,000 to 125,000 and doubles the number of men drafted per month from 17,000 to 35,000.

- In response to events in Montgomery, Ala., President Johnson proposes the Voting Rights Act of 1965. It becomes law in August.

- Students for a Democratic Society (SDS) hold a "teach-in" against the Vietnam War at the University of Michigan; 2,500 people participate. An SDS protest later in the year brings 25,000 protestors to Washington, D.C. Still later that year, anti-war protests draw 100,000 people in 80 U.S. cities and around the world.

- The Social Security Act of 1965 is enacted. The Act establishes Medicare and Medicaid.

- The Watts Riots erupt and rage for six days in Los Angeles.

- Fidel Castro announces that anyone who wants can immigrate to the U.S. In October, the first Cuban refugees arrive. In November, Freedom Flights begin. By 1971, 250,000 Cubans take advantage of this program.

- Popular movies: *The Flight of the Phoenix, The Sound of Music, Juliet of the Spirits.*

- Popular songs: *(I Can't Get No) Satisfaction, I Can't Help Myself, Wooly Bully.*

- Popular TV shows: *Flipper, Gilligan's Island, The Andy Griffith Show.*

- Popular books: *The Source,* James Michener; *Up the Down Staircase,* Bel Kaufman; *Herzog,* Saul Bellow.

- Average annual U.S. family income: $6,900.

The same year, the Medicare Act was passed, which combined hospital insurance for retired people with a voluntary plan to cover physicians' bills. Medicaid provided grants to states to help provide medical care to lower-income people. Legislation for education, immigration and housing passed in 1965.

In March, Dr. Martin Luther King Jr. announced a voter registration drive and led a march from Selma to Montgomery, Ala. At the time, 70 percent of African-Americans lived in ghettos across the country. The marchers were stopped by police, and 50 were hospitalized when police used tear gas, whips and clubs on them. The march and ensuing clash with police became known as "Bloody Sunday" and was a catalyst for pushing the Voting Rights Act through Congress five months later. The legislation, quickly signed into law by President Johnson, guaranteed federal protections of the right to register and vote.

At the same time, race riots exploded around the country, beginning with Los Angeles in 1965 and followed by New York City and Chicago in 1966, and Newark, N.J., and Detroit in 1967, among others. According to the Kerner

ASPA SNAPSHOT

- Two new publications are launched: the *Washington Newsletter* and *What's New*. The *Washington Newsletter* features information about legislation affecting the field and is mailed at irregular intervals to all Society members. *What's New* features Society news. *ASPA Action*, the publication to replace *Leaders Forum*, is also launched and sent to all members every two months.

- The Fort Collins, Colo., office closes when it is decided to publish *The Personnel Administrator* from the Berea, Ohio, office in anticipation of the retirement of the magazine's editor, Ray Davies. Willard Largent is hired as editor on a part-time basis.

- The Annual Conference is held in Omaha, Neb.

- Conference attendance: 333.

- Conference surplus: $4,141.86.

- Membership: 3,322.

- Committees: 22.

- Annual budget: $77,750.

- Reserves: $29,319.34.

Commission, the riots were aimed at a social system that prevented African-Americans from good jobs and crowded them into ghettos. African-American radicals and other urban revolutionaries began to emerge: Stokely Carmichael, H. Rap Brown, Huey Newton and Bobby Seale founded the Black Panthers in 1966. And more ethnic activism emerged. For example, Cesar Chavez and the United Farm Workers' Organizing Committee conducted a successful California grape pickers strike that lasted five years. The American Indian Movement, or AIM, began gathering support around the country.

In September, President Johnson issued Executive Order 11246, which enforced affirmative action for the first time. The order required government contractors to take affirmative action toward prospective minority employees in all aspects of hiring and employment and established the Office of Federal Contract Compliance Programs, better known as the OFCCP. The executive order also required contractors to conduct and document specific actions to ensure equality in hiring. In October 1967, the order was amended to cover gender discrimination.

Other major societal issues began to boil over. The first substantial U.S. bombing—Rolling Thunder—took place in Vietnam. By 1968, 538,000 U.S. troops were deployed in Vietnam.

The January/February 1965 issue of *The Personnel Administrator* featured articles such as "Performance Appraisal as a Supervisory Tool," "Employment Turns to Computers," "Personnel Management—One of the Black Arts" and "Grievance Handling is the Job of a Supervisor."

1966 WORLD EVENTS

- The National Organization for Women is formed.
- A U.S. Supreme Court ruling establishes Miranda Rights.
- The Black Panthers are formed.
- China's Cultural Revolution starts.
- The first episode of *Star Trek* airs.
- Popular movies: *Thunderball, Dr. Zhivago, Who's Afraid of Virginia Woolf?*
- Popular songs: *I'm a Believer, Good Vibrations, Monday Monday.*
- Popular TV shows: *Star Trek, Batman, The Monkees.*
- Popular books: *Valley of the Dolls*, Jacqueline Susann; *In Cold Blood*, Truman Capote; *The Adventurers*, Harold Robbins.
- Average annual U.S. family income: $7,400.

In 1966, the National Organization for Women was established, calling for equal employment opportunities and equal pay for women. The Equal Rights Amendment failed because abortion rights issues incensed the right-to-life movement.

While massive changes were taking place in the world around it, the ASPA Board looked to expand services to members that reflected what was going on in the country. It agreed to a cooperative survey on maternity leave with Prentice-Hall, a significant event in light of a recent ruling by the Equal Employment Opportunity Commission (EEOC) that required employers to treat maternity leaves as leaves of absence with no break in seniority.

That year, the Society also sponsored a survey with the Manpower Research Council on national job availability,

ASPA SNAPSHOT

- The ASPA Foundation's Wisconsin incorporation is terminated, and plans are made to incorporate the foundation in Ohio. The reorganization allows the foundation to have an elected board and more control over funds and activities.
- The affiliate membership class is discontinued.
- The Annual Conference is held in Miami Beach, Fla.
- Conference attendance: 582.
- Conference surplus: $6,586.
- Membership: 3,787.
- Chapters: 85.
- Committees: 28.
- Staff: Seven (three full time and four part time).
- Annual budget: $84,500.
- Reserves: $33,409.53.

which it believed would provide insight into manpower needs for the future. The Society also planned to launch a joint program with the Bureau of National Affairs in 1967. The joint program would design and provide presentations on labor relations, the Fair Labor Standards Act, unemployment compensation and the EEOC.

The ASPA Board also began to discuss issues of discrimination in the workplace and aiding and assisting soldiers returning from Vietnam by offering career counseling support. In 1967, the Age Discrimination in Employment Act made it illegal for employers to discriminate against anyone over the age of 40 with respect to hiring, firing, promotion, compensation, benefits, job assignments and training.

The Board of Directors also recognized the need for a means to accept donations and provide grants to educational institutions and researchers. Even though ASPA had established a foundation years earlier, in 1966 the Board amended the bylaws to create a new ASPA Foundation and incorporate the new entity in Ohio.

ASPA's first president, Walter Mason, was named the foundation's first president. Robert L. Berra, SPHR, ASPA's president in 1968, said, "It really was a matter of putting our money where our mouth was. The time was right to create an arm where the Society could fund research projects and scholarships. ASPA had to do this if we wanted to be considered the leading organization in the HR profession."

During this time, ASPA began to make inroads toward establishing strong international relationships. It agreed to pay for its executive vice president, Leonard Brice, to attend the 1967 Council for International Progress in Management, which was held in Rotterdam in the Netherlands. ASPA's International Affairs Committee, chaired by Bert Walters, had established relationships with other personnel administration organizations in Canada, England, France and Spain. Board members had also reached out to colleagues in Tokyo and Hong Kong. And ASPA had been invited to attend the Marseilles International Conference in France and the Latin American Conference in Venezuela.

1967 WORLD EVENTS

- Arab forces attack Israel to begin the Yom Kippur War. The Egyptian and Syrian forces are defeated quickly, and Israel takes possession of additional territory in the Sinai Peninsula and on the Syrian border. This becomes known as the Six Day War.
- The Organization of Petroleum Exporting Countries (OPEC) announces an oil embargo to countries that supported Israel.
- Race riots break out in a number of U.S. cities, including Cleveland; Newark, N.J.; and Detroit.
- China tests its first hydrogen bomb.
- Popular movies: *The Dirty Dozen, You Only Live Twice, Casino Royale.*
- Popular songs: *To Sir with Love, Happy Together, Windy.*
- Popular TV shows: *The Prisoner, The Forsyte Saga, Coronation Street.*
- Popular books: *The Arrangement*, Elia Kazan; *The Confessions of Nat Turner*, William Styron; *The Chosen*, Chaim Potok.
- Average annual U.S. family income: $8,000.

Racial tensions continued to build in the U.S. In April, Stokely Carmichael coined the phrase "black power." His radicalism and influence worried many in the civil rights movement, including Dr. Martin Luther King Jr., who believed that progress depended on nonviolent civil disobedience. Pervasive discrimination and segregation in employment, education and housing continued. Poverty was an overwhelming issue for nonwhites.

The feminist movement was reflected in the Society's magazine, *The Personnel Administrator*. In the early 1960s, advertisements urged readers to "Use Gals from Manpower as Temporary Vacation Replacements," and an advertisement for a newsletter called *Just Between Office Girls* read "Your Office Girls Need Lovin' Care." By 1967, one advertisement proclaimed "Marilyn Ross is No Girl." There was still a long way to go, but it was a start.

ASPA and the Cornell University School of Industrial Relations co-sponsored a three-day conference that year to discuss certification for the profession and to try to define the profession's common body of knowledge. According to Bill Leonard's 1998 history of the Society in *HR Magazine*, the conference was pretty intense. In fact, in a 1975 article for *The Personnel Administrator*, Wiley Beaver wrote, "We parted as friends—in some cases just barely—and I, for one, considered accreditation to be a dead issue." He would be proved wrong.

ASPA continued to grow, adding more than $8,000 to reserves between 1966 and 1967. Conference attendance reached its highest level to date, as did the conference surplus. Thirteen new chapters were added, including the Puerto Rico chapter, the first chapter established outside of the United States.

Fifteen Freedom Riders who arrived on a second bus in Jackson, Miss., are loaded into a paddy wagon at the bus station, May 24, 1961. (AP Photo/Horace Cort)

1968 WORLD EVENTS

- French students take to the streets in Paris in support of workers who went on strike to protest wages, bringing the city to a virtual standstill. Fighting breaks out between students and police. The minimum wage is raised by 35 percent, and the government restores order.

- On April 4, Dr. Martin Luther King Jr. is assassinated in Memphis, Tenn.

- On June 5, Robert F. Kennedy is assassinated in Los Angeles by Sirhan Sirhan.

- 700 protestors are injured and 650 arrested after violence breaks out outside of the Democratic Convention in Chicago. The event is widely covered on television.

- Richard M. Nixon is elected president.

- The Civil Rights Act of 1968 is signed into law.

- Communists launch the Tet Offensive in Vietnam.

- Popular movies: *The Graduate, Guess Who's Coming to Dinner, The Jungle Book*.

- Popular songs: *Hey Jude, Honey, Love is Blue*.

- Popular TV shows: *Laugh-In, Here's Lucy, Mayberry R.F.D.*

- Popular books: *Airport*, Arthur Hailey; *Couples*, John Updike; *The Salzburg Connection*, Helen MacInnes.

- Average annual U.S. family income: $8,630.

In 2003, Mark Kurlansky wrote a book with a title that pretty much sums up the year: *1968: The Year that Rocked the World*. Television brought the Vietnam War, the French student protests, the assassinations of Dr. Martin Luther King Jr. and Robert F. Kennedy, and the feminist movement directly into the living rooms of American families.

By 1968, 3 million African-Americans had registered to vote in the South. Congress passed the Civil Rights Act of 1968, which prohibited discrimination in the sale,

ASPA SNAPSHOT

- First board meeting of the newly formed ASPA Foundation is held. The Board consists of Walter Mason, president; Paul E. Jacobs, vice president; and Leonard Brice, secretary/treasurer.

- *What's New* discontinues publication.

- The Annual Conference is held in Philadelphia.

- Conference attendance: 425.

- Conference registration fees: $50 for members, $60 for nonmembers and $40 for wives.

- Conference surplus: $7,175.53.

- Membership: 4,302.

- Chapters: 96.

- Committees: 25.

- Staff: eight (four full time and four part time).

- Annual budget: $104,200.

- Reserves: $41,566.

rental and financing of housing. In April, Dr. King was killed in Memphis, Tenn., and Kennedy was assassinated a few short months later in Los Angeles—after he won the California primary and became the leading contender for the Democratic Party's nomination for president.

North Vietnam launched the Tet Offensive against U.S. forces across South Vietnam on January 3, and the bitter fighting prompted many Americans to change their opinion and oppose the war. College and university demonstrations against the war became almost commonplace as students also began protesting against the government bureaucracy and showed their support for civil rights. Students at Columbia University in New York City staged a sit-in blocking entrance to the university's administration building, closing down the school for several days. The hippie counterculture took hold, as did women's liberation.

President Johnson signed an executive order banning sex discrimination in federally connected employment. More than 1,000 lawsuits charging sexual discrimination were initiated by the National Organization for Women against U.S. corporations. The Equal Employment Opportunity Commission ruled that sex-segregated want ads in newspapers were illegal, and the ruling was upheld in 1973 by the Supreme Court.

Through all this turmoil, leaders of ASPA looked at ways to better define the HR profession. ASPA and Cornell University held a follow-up meeting to the 1967 conference on certification. During that meeting, it was agreed that a profession needed to have:

- School curricula aimed specifically at educating students about the profession, with a defined common body of knowledge.

- A code of ethics.

- A national professional association.

- A certification or credentialing program.

"We agreed that the HR profession at that time met all the criteria except the defined body of knowledge and the certification program," said Drew Young, SPHR, who attended the meeting and later served as ASPA president in 1970. The Board would establish a task force on accreditation in 1972, and in 1973 the ASPA accreditation program was born.

ASPA celebrated its 20th anniversary during this history-making year. Its focus remained on advancing the personnel profession and on providing cutting-edge information to its members. Although there were now 10 employees in the Berea, Ohio, office, the Society's backbone remained its volunteers, with consistently more than 20 committees operating each year. For the landmark anniversary, ASPA set an ambitious membership goal to reach 5,000 members. The goal was surpassed by year's end, when membership totaled 5,410 professional and student members.

1969 WORLD EVENTS

- After 147 years, the last issue of *The Saturday Evening Post* is published.
- The Beatles give their last public performance on the rooftop of Apple Records.

ASPA SNAPSHOT

- ❖ ASPA celebrates its 20th anniversary.
- ❖ The Annual Conference is held in Denver. Attendance is 649.
- ❖ Membership: 5,410.
- ❖ Chapters: 110.
- ❖ Staff: 10 (seven full time and three part time).
- ❖ Annual budget: $133,775.
- ❖ Reserves: $48,473.
- ❖ ASPA Foundation reserves: $7,629.26.

ASPA SNAPSHOT

- ❖ In January, ASPA and the Bureau of National Affairs (BNA) form the ASPA/BNA Council. This "blue ribbon" advisory council of approximately 250 ASPA members assists BNA in joint survey projects, with the results published by BNA.
- ❖ Membership dues are increased from $25 for regular and associate members to $30. The increase will go into effect in 1971.
- ❖ The Annual Conference is held in Atlanta; 966 members attend.
- ❖ Membership: 6,696.
- ❖ Annual budget: $160,000.

- The first test flight of the Concorde supersonic passenger plane is conducted in Toulouse, France.
- The Harvard University administration building is seized by Students for a Democratic Society. By the end of the takeover, 45 people are injured and 184 arrested.
- John Lennon releases the hit song *Give Peace a Chance*.
- On July 8, the first U.S. troop withdrawals begin in Vietnam.
- Apollo 11 lands on the moon. Neil Armstrong becomes the first man to walk on the moon.
- In August, nearly 500,000 people attend the Woodstock Rock Festival in upstate New York.
- Popular movies: *The Love Bug, Funny Girl, Butch Cassidy and the Sundance Kid*.
- Popular songs: *Crimson and Clover, Everyday People, Dizzy*.
- Popular TV shows: *Laugh-In, Gunsmoke, Bonanza*.
- Popular books: *Portnoy's Complaint*, Philip Roth; *The Godfather*, Mario Puzo; *The Love Machine*, Jacqueline Susann.
- Average annual U.S. family income: $9,430.

By 1969, women had become 40 percent of the U.S. labor force, with large numbers serving as secretaries, cleaning women, elementary school teachers, saleswomen, waitresses and nurses. Women in the workplace were subjected to insults, sexual jokes and aggression, and invisibility except as sexual objects. ASPA was engaged in exploring a research project with Catalyst in the area of using college graduate wives and mothers in part-time jobs in business and industry.

ASPA continued is own evolution, hosting its most-attended conference to date. In 1969, new aims and objectives were approved for the Society.

The revised aims and objectives were:

- To provide assistance in the professional development of every member.

- To provide national leadership in establishing and supporting standards of excellence in every phase of Personnel—Industrial Relations—Manpower Management.

- To provide the impetus for research needed in the Personnel—Industrial Relations—Manpower Management field.

- To serve as a focal point for the exchange of authoritative data and information.

- To publicize Relations—Manpower Management field to assure a better understanding of its functions, responsibilities and importance.

RECAP OF KEY EVENTS IN HUMAN RESOURCE MANAGEMENT

1960–1969

1963	The Equal Pay Act is enacted.
1964	ASPA headquarters opens in Berea, Ohio.
1964	Title VII of the Civil Rights Act is enacted.
1965	Leonard Brice, SPHR, becomes head of ASPA staff as executive vice president.
1965	President Johnson signs Affirmative Action Executive Order 11246.
1965	Medicare and Medicaid are established.
1966	A new ASPA Foundation is established.
1967	The Age Discrimination in Employment Act (ADEA) is enacted.
1969	ASPA membership reaches 6,696.

1970s

ASPA SNAPSHOT

- The phrase "human resource management" first appears in the May/June issue of *The Personnel Administrator* in an article by 1970 ASPA President Drew Young, SPHR.

- The ASPA Foundation receives its first industry grant of $1,000 from Bristol-Myers. ASPA contributes $5,000 to the foundation, bringing total foundation receipts to $15,414.

- The ASPA Board approves computerization of the national office.

- The Annual Conference is held in San Francisco.

- Conference attendance: 1,152, surpassing 1,000 for the first time.

- Conference surplus: $16,863.

- Membership: 7,943.

- Chapters: 145 (140 professional chapters and five student chapters).

- Committees: 29.

- Annual budget: $209,500 (nearly 31 percent more than in 1969).

- Reserves: $58,295.

It seemed that the chaos of the 1960s would continue into the 1970s. Anti-war demonstrations, civil rights and integration, and the women's movement were all gaining steam. As the decade wore on, Watergate, the oil embargo and one of the worst recessions in 40 years caused the American public to lose faith in business, government and religion. According to the University of Michigan Survey Research Center, trust in government was low in every section of the population. In 1964, when asked if the government was run by a few big interests looking out for themselves, 26 percent of American citizens answered yes. By 1972, 53 percent of Americans replied yes to the same question.

ASPA continued to flourish. By the time the first HR professional was certified by ASPA Accreditation Institute in 1976, the Society had a budget of more than $700,000, nearly 20,000 members and a staff of 19.

1970 WORLD EVENTS

- The first Earth Day is celebrated, and the environmental movement begins.
- In May, four students are killed by National Guard troops during an anti-war demonstration at Kent State University.
- The World Trade Center is completed in New York City.

- The floppy disk is invented.
- 18-year-olds are given the right to vote.
- The Occupational Safety and Health Administration is established.
- 31 percent of American workers are union members.
- Popular movies: *Love Story, M*A*S*H, Chariots of the Gods.*
- Popular songs: *Bridge Over Troubled Water, (They Long to Be) Close to You, American Woman.*
- Popular TV shows: *Marcus Welby, M.D.; The Flip Wilson Show; Ironside.*
- Popular books: *Love Story*, Erich Segal; *The French Lieutenant's Woman*, John Fowles; *Islands in the Stream*, Ernest Hemingway.
- Average annual U.S. family income: $9,870.

By 1970, the average life expectancy of Americans had increased to 71 years, 18-year-olds were given the right to vote, and an energy crisis gripped the country. U.S. troops invaded Cambodia, and at Kent State University in Ohio, four students were killed protesting the ongoing war.

In *Schultz vs. Wheaton Glass Co.*, a U.S. Court of Appeals ruled that jobs held by men and women needed to be "substantially equal" but not identical to fall under the Equal Pay Act. An employer could not, for example, change the job titles of female workers in order to pay them less than men.

U.S. Paratroopers dash from helicopters in the jungle clearing in War Zone C during an assault on suspected Viet Cong positions about 65 miles northwest of Saigon in South Vietnam as part of Operation Junction City during the Vietnam War on March 8, 1967. (AP Photo/Horst Faas)

The Occupational Safety and Health Administration (OSHA) was established amid concerns about the environmental health of organizations and injuries to employees.

Although ASPA now had 12 employees at the national office, the Society continued to be driven in large part by its extensive volunteer structure; there were 29 working committees that year, and the ASPA Board had 42 members. Volunteers continued to fine-tune the regional structure, moving Bermuda from Region VII to Region II. The Board also approved a bylaws change and created a retired member classification.

Efforts to improve the quality of the profession were also continuing. The ASPA Board struck a deal with Florida Atlantic University to offer ASPA members the opportunity to participate in a three-year program and earn a master's degree in business administration through the university. The MBA program veered off the traditional education route and required students to spend only five weeks each year on campus. The balance of the academic year was spent in home study.

This was a landmark year for technology because the first interchangeable computer memory disk—fondly known as the floppy disk—was invented. That same year, the ASPA Board of Directors approved the computerization of the national office, which was a pretty forward-thinking move. The Society would show its technological savvy again in the early 1990s, when its successor organization, the Society for Human Resource Management, became one of the first associations to establish an online presence.

ASPA hires a part-time lobbyist to represent its interests in Congress.

By June 1971, ASPA agreed to finance a part-time Washington representative, Robert Borth, who was hired to communicate legislative and regulatory information to ASPA members 10 times a year.

The Board also moved that ASPA bylaws be amended to allow that full-time consultants and regular members could chair national committees (they were not eligible, however, to hold national elective office) and that employment agency practitioners be classified as associate members. In another move, the Board agreed that the Pacific Northwest Personnel Management Association would officially affiliate with ASPA on January 1, 1972.

ASPA SNAPSHOT

- The membership dues increase (to $30) goes into effect.

- The subscription fee for *The Personnel Administrator* is increased to $10 per year.

- Twenty-nine chapters affiliate, for a total of 159 professional chapters and 14 student chapters.

- The Board approves the affiliation of the Pacific Northwest Personnel Management Association, effective January 1, 1972.

- The Annual Conference is held in Dallas.

- Conference attendance: 804.

- Conference registration fees: $75 for members and $105 for nonmembers.

- Conference surplus: $12,515.

- Membership: 8,702.

- Committees: 31.

- Staff: 12 (10 full time and two part time).

- Annual budget: $300,900.

- Reserves: $70,521.

1972 **WORLD EVENTS**

- President Nixon visits China and meets with Mao Zedong.

- The Watergate scandal erupts. The scandal ultimately leads to President Nixon's resignation.

- Eleven Israeli athletes are killed by Palestinian terrorists during the Olympic Summer Games in Munich, West Germany.

- Congress agrees to send the Equal Rights Amendment to the states for ratification.

- The first female FBI agents are hired.

- Shirley Chisholm, the first African-American congresswoman, becomes a candidate for president. She wins 162 delegates.

- The first hand-held scientific calculator is introduced. Cost: $395.

- Popular movies: *The Godfather, Cabaret, Deliverance.*

- Popular songs: *The First Time Ever I Saw Your Face, Alone Again (Naturally), American Pie.*

- Popular TV shows: *Hawaii Five-O, Maude, Bridget Loves Bernie.*

- Popular books: *Jonathan Livingston Seagull,* Richard Bach; *The Word,* Irving Wallace; *The Winds of War,* Herman Wouk.

- Average annual U.S. family income: $11,120.

The merger with the Pacific Northwest Personnel Management Association raised ASPA membership above the 10,000 mark, a major milestone for the Society. Conference attendance was also strong, with more than 1,000 people attending the conference in Boston. Conference sessions included "The Employment of Homosexuals," "Drug Use and Industry," "The Flexible Workweek and New Horizons to Explore," "The Labor Movement and the New Work Force," and "Changing Moral Attitudes and the Women's Lib Movement."

The Society also introduced a revised code of ethics that year:

ASPA: **Code of Ethics**

As a member of the American Society for Personnel Administration, I acknowledge my responsibility to strive for personal growth in my chosen career field and commit myself to observe the following ethical practices:

- I will respect the dignity of the individual as one of the essential elements of success in any enterprise.

- I will demonstrate and promote a spirit of cooperative effort between owners, managers, employees and the general public, directly or indirectly connected with the enterprise.

- I will advance those ethical employee relations concepts in personnel administration and labor relations, which contribute to the objectives of the enterprise.

- I will reveal the facts in any situation where my private interests are in conflict with those of my employer or other principals.

- I will not permit considerations of religion, nationality, race, sex, age, party politics or social standings to influence my professional activities.

- I will strive to attain and demonstrate a professional level of competence within the body of knowledge comprising the management field.

ASPA SNAPSHOT

- ⬥ ASPA establishes a Washington, D.C., legislative office.
- ⬥ The Pacific Northwest Personnel Management Association becomes an ASPA chapter.
- ⬥ ASPA approves a new code of ethics.
- ⬥ The Annual Conference is held in Boston.
- ⬥ Conference attendance: 1,134.
- ⬥ Membership: 10,453.
- ⬥ Chapters: 211 (186 professional chapters and 25 student chapters).
- ⬥ Committees: 29.
- ⬥ Board members: 42.
- ⬥ Staff: 13 (11 full time and two part time).
- ⬥ Annual budget: $338,900.
- ⬥ Reserves: $81,342.

- I will encourage and participate in research to develop and advance new and improved management methods, skills and practices, sharing the productive results of such research with others.

- I will never use the Society or its membership for purposes other than those for which they were designed.

1973 WORLD EVENTS

- A cease-fire signed on January 28 ends the U.S. involvement in the Vietnam War.
- President Nixon accepts responsibility (but not the blame) for Watergate.
- Vice President Spiro Agnew resigns and pleads no contest to charges of tax evasion.
- The Supreme Court rules on *Roe vs. Wade*.
- Popular movies: *The Exorcist, Serpico, American Graffiti.*
- Popular songs: *Tie a Yellow Ribbon 'Round the Ole Oak Tree, Bad Bad Leroy Brown, Killing Me Softly with His Song.*
- Popular TV shows: *The Waltons, Kojak, The Mary Tyler Moore Show.*
- Popular books: *Breakfast of Champions,* Kurt Vonnegut; *The Matlock Paper,* Robert Ludlum; *Dr. Atkins' Diet Revolution,* Robert C. Atkins.
- Average annual U.S. family income: $12,050.

The year that ASPA celebrated its 25th anniversary, the nation remained in turmoil. President Nixon abolished the draft, while congressional hearings of the Watergate scandal began. In the landmark *Roe vs. Wade* decision, the Supreme Court decided that: 1) the government could prohibit abortions only in the last three months of pregnancy; 2) the government could regulate abortion for health purposes during the second trimester; and 3)

during the first three months, a woman and her doctor had the right to decide.

Congress still showed an interest in workplace legislation and enacted the Rehabilitation Act, which continued a federal vocational rehabilitation program for people with disabilities. The law also included provisions that prohibited federal agencies and federal contractors from discriminating against job applicants or employees with disabilities.

The ASPA Board of Directors made a huge leap forward in creating a professional certification program when it voted to approve an accreditation for HR and appointed a task force to explore the possibilities of creating a nationwide program.

Later in 1973, the Board discussed a possible name change for the Society, an issue that had come up several times before. ASPA Executive Vice President Leonard Brice, SPHR, discussed the subject with the Board, noting that ASPA was becoming more international and that "human resource management" was fast becoming the term to use instead of personnel administration. He suggested the name The Council of Human Resources Management. The Board did not agree to change the name, but it did amend the bylaws to remove the words "in America."

The 25th Annual Conference was held in Puerto Rico that year. It was the first and only time that the Society's annual meeting was held outside the continental United States. Although the Board rejected the name change suggested by Brice, the conference theme, "Advancing Human Resource Management to Meet Changing Life Styles," did reflect a trend in changing terminology and indicated the direction the Society was headed.

ASPA SNAPSHOT

- The ASPA Board approves a certification for practitioners in the personnel field and appoints a task force to explore the possibility.

- The 25th Annual Conference is held in San Juan, Puerto Rico. It is the first ASPA conference held outside the United States.

- Conference attendance: 1,278.

- Conference surplus: $4,467.

- Membership: 12,268.

- Chapters: 234 (197 professional chapters and 37 student chapters).

- Committees: 25.

- Board members: 43.

- Annual budget: $387,700.

- Reserves: $124,147.

In 1973, for the first time in its history, ASPA filed a position paper on legislation pending in Congress and provided testimony before a congressional committee. ASPA officials chose to set this groundbreaking precedent on a landmark piece of legislation that has had a huge impact on HR professionals today—the Employee Retirement Income Security Act (ERISA). The position paper secured ASPA's involvement in ongoing discussions to understand and implement the provisions of ERISA that continue even today.

1974 WORLD EVENTS

- Ethiopian Emperor Haile Selassie is deposed by military leaders after ruling for 44 years.

- U.S. inflation rates hit 12 percent following the oil crisis.

- On August 9, President Nixon resigns to avoid impeachment. Vice President Gerald Ford becomes the 38th president. Ford later pardons Nixon.

- The Symbionese Liberation Army kidnaps Patricia Hearst, granddaughter of publishing and movie mogul William Randolph Hearst.

- Hank Aaron breaks Babe Ruth's home run record.

- World population tops 4 billion.

- Popular movies: *Chinatown, The Longest Yard, Blazing Saddles.*

- Popular songs: *The Way We Were, Seasons in the Sun, Dancing Machine.*

- Popular TV shows: *Chico and the Man, The Jeffersons, M*A*S*H.*

- Popular books: *All the President's Men,* Carl Bernstein and Bob Woodward; *Centennial,* James A. Michener; *Watership Down,* Richard Adams.

- Average annual U.S. family income: $12,840.

In 1974, oil-exporting Arabic nations declared an oil boycott of the United States. The Arabs later lifted the boycott, but OPEC—the Organization of Petroleum Exporting Countries, which included Venezuela, Saudi Arabia, Kuwait, Iraq and Iran—raised the price of oil from $3 per barrel to $11.65 per barrel. Gas prices in the U.S. doubled, and inflation sharply increased to 12 percent.

In September, ERISA, which imposed new federal standards and regulations on employer-provided benefits plans, took effect. The law was designed to protect the security of retirement benefits offered by private-sector employers.

Congress wasn't the only branch of government that was having a major impact on the HR profession and the U.S. workplace. In *Corning Glass Works vs. Brennan,* the Supreme Court ruled that employers could not justify paying women lower wages because that is what they traditionally received under the "going market rate." Around this same time, the U.S. Census Bureau estimated that there were approximately 54,000 personnel professionals in the U.S. earning $15,000 or more annually.

In recognition of the proliferation of workplace laws and legislation, ASPA's Long-Range Planning Committee recommended that the Society employ a full-time Washington representative and a director of professional development. The Board agreed to fill both positions by the end of 1975.

ASPA also began discussions about creating a world federation for the personnel profession. ASPA representatives met with Raul Caldiera, president of the European Personnel Association (EAPM), and the Board approved exploring the possibility of founding an international federation with EAPM.

The final issue of *The Personnel Administrator* of 1974 called for ASPA members to communicate directly with their legislators. "Businessmen must establish better contact with their elected representatives if they expect to be listened to," wrote Joseph T. Bailey, chairman and president of the Warner and Swansey Company of Cleveland. He instructed readers to be willing to compromise, to be reasonable and, above all, not to threaten.

1975 WORLD EVENTS

- U.S. Attorney General John Mitchell and former White House aides H.R. Haldeman and John Ehrlichman are found guilty in the Watergate scandal.

- The Vietnam War ends on April 30, as communist forces take Saigon.

- Bill Gates launches Microsoft.

- *Saturday Night Live* debuts.

- An audit of Mattel, one of the largest toy manufacturers in the U.S., shows that corporate leaders fabricated press releases and financial information to maintain an appearance of continued growth.

- Minimum wage increases to $2.10 per hour.

- Popular movies: *One Flew Over the Cuckoo's Nest, Jaws, Dog Day Afternoon.*

- Popular songs: *Love Will Keep Us Together, Rhinestone Cowboy, Philadelphia Freedom.*

- Popular TV shows: *Happy Days; Laverne & Shirley; Welcome Back, Kotter.*

- Popular books: *Ragtime,* E.L. Doctorow; *Looking for Mr. Goodbar,* Judith Rossner; *Winning through Intimidation,* Robert Ringer.

- Average annual U.S. family income: $13,720.

In W.H. Miller's history of ASPA, 1975 is the first year that he acknowledged the potential effect of current events on the Society; he noted that the "serious business recession" could present challenges for the Society in terms of membership growth and general Society advancement. According to Miller, ASPA President George Rieder "had planned his 1975 operation well and was ready immediately at the start of his term for positive action."

And the ASPA Board did act, moving to protect the Society's financial position. Following Board approval in 1974, membership dues were raised to $40 for regular and associate members, and subscription fees for *The Personnel Administrator* were adjusted with a higher fee for nonmembers residing outside the U.S. and U.S. territories. Conference registration fees were also increased, from $115 for nonmembers to $125. The conference cleared more than $25,000 that year, and conference registration exceeded the previous year by more than 100 attendees. Forty-nine chapters affiliated with the Society, although the goal of having 252 professional and 85 student chapters was not realized. The ambitious membership goal of 18,300 was also not met. Despite these setbacks, the Society was still able to set aside money to reserves during a severe recession.

The Society was not only making strides in growing its chapter and membership networks, it was also busy fulfilling its long-term strategic goals. The ASPA Accreditation Institute was formed, and in just one short year, it would offer its first certification exam. By ASPA Board approval, the accreditation program would be run by an organization separate from the Society. It was initially called the PAIRA Institute but would eventually be called the ASPA Accreditation Institute and then later

ASPA SNAPSHOT

- The ASPA Accreditation Institute is formed.

- A student newsletter is launched, with the first issue published in April.

- The Annual Conference is held in Orlando, Fla.

- Conference attendance: 1,501.

- Conference exhibitors: 62.

- Conference surplus: $25,486.

- Membership: 16,919.

- Chapters: 310 (233 professional chapters and 77 student chapters).

- Committees: 23.

- Board members: 43.

- Staff: 19 (16 full time and three part time).

- Annual budget: $597,900.

- Reserves: $200,971.

renamed the Personnel Accreditation Institute (PAI). In 1990, the institute was renamed again to the Human Resource Certification Institute, and in 2008 it became the HR Certification Institute.

In addition to the formation of an accreditation body, ASPA submitted three amicus briefs to the U.S. Supreme Court; filed an average of one position paper every two weeks in Washington, D.C., with the top issues being the Employee Retirement Income Security Act, national health insurance, unemployment, the Occupational Safety and Health Act, wage and price controls, and the Equal Employment Opportunity Commission; placed "image building" articles in leading professional publications; conducted 27 seminars and co-sponsored 12 more with the Bureau of National Affairs; and agreed that in light of affirmative action, the bylaws should be reviewed to ensure that any sex bias had been eliminated.

1975 was the first year that Board minutes reflected a concern about the lack of minority and female representation on the Board and among the Society's volunteer leaders. A task force was assigned to study the issue and make recommendations to the Board.

The Personnel Administrator reflected the increasing presence of women in the workplace. 1975 was "International Women's Year," and in April, one article looked at "Keys to Success or Failure" for female managers. Another article addressed "de-sexing the language" and provided a few examples of what not to say, including "I'll have my girl do it," "career girl" and "the best man for the job." An article by Rieder referred to a manager as "he or she."

The ASPA Board was also becoming more concerned about providing exemplary personnel management for the headquarters staff. It approved the formation of a standing committee of the Board to work with the executive vice president on the design and implementation of personnel policies and practices for headquarters staff and the selection of key professional staff.

Discussions about the formation of the World Federation of Personnel Management Associations (WFPMA) also continued; ASPA Executive Vice President Leonard Brice traveled to Brussels, Belgium, to participate in the discussions. The South American Personnel Association also approached ASPA about joining its organization, FIDAP. ASPA delayed a decision on joining until the WFPMA tie-in was established.

The Board also agreed to issue the following statement about the threat of another wage-price freeze (President Nixon had issued a six-month price freeze during his administration):

As a professional society of over 14,000 personnel and industrial relations practitioners whose careers are dedicated to maximizing our human resources in employment, the American Society for Personnel Administration is deeply concerned over the persistent reports emanating from our nation's capital over the possible reactivation of wage and price controls.

Apprehension over the reinstitution of controls, if not expeditiously and forcefully dispelled, is likely to dangerously aggravate the serious joblessness and inflation that already besets our economy as both unions and companies seek to hedge against the possibility of controls with anticipatory wage and price actions.

The severe repercussions reactivation of controls would visit on the job marketplace and our economic structure can be measured in part by our experience from 1971–1974, when

- serious wage and salary inequities were created between unionized and non-unionized employees;

- profit limitations led to reduced production, shortages and layoffs; and

- advantageous price differentials for foreign buyers caused more domestic shortages and layoffs.

Although we are greatly encouraged by the fact that the Administration has presently opted to avoid wage-price controls as a part of its new economic policy, apprehension over the possibility of their reactivation is likely to continue absent a clear and firm expression of agreement with that policy decision by the Congress.

Wage-price controls make no sense.

It makes even less sense for the Congress to fail to act early and forcefully to dispel the widespread apprehension of their adoption. Only then will artificial forces that will serve to jeopardize our nation's early return to a healthy economy be eliminated.

The adoption of a resolution expressing the sense of the Congress against the reactivation of wage and price controls should be one of the first priorities of the 94th Congress.

Jimmy Carter takes the oath of office as the nation's 39th president during inauguration ceremonies in Washington, D.C., on Jan. 20, 1977. (AP Photo)

1976 WORLD EVENTS

- The U.S. celebrates its bicentennial.
- The U.S. Supreme Court rules that African-Americans and other minorities are entitled to retroactive job seniority.
- The U.S. Naval Academy in Annapolis, Md., inducts its first class with women.
- The first recognized outbreak of Legionnaires' disease kills 29 people during an American Legion convention in Philadelphia.
- Jimmy Carter is elected president, defeating incumbent Gerald Ford.
- Apple Computer is formed by Steve Jobs and Steve Wozniak.
- Popular movies: *All the President's Men, Rocky, Taxi Driver.*
- Popular songs: *Silly Love Songs, Don't Go Breaking My Heart, December 1963 (Oh What a Night).*
- Popular TV shows: *Charlie's Angels, The Six Million Dollar Man, Three's Company.*
- Popular books: *Trinity,* Leon Uris; *1876,* Gore Vidal; *Roots,* Alex Haley.
- Average annual U.S. family income: $14,960.

At the January 1976 Board meeting, John Blodger, SPHR, was named treasurer. He was the first African-American to serve as part of the executive committee. In addition, two women—Catherine Hildeen and Helen Saylor—were also named to the executive committee.

The Board approved the creation of the World Federation of Personnel Management Associations and its bylaws. ASPA was the last affiliating national group. The signing ceremony for the WFPMA took place during the ASPA conference, with representatives from the European Personnel Association, FIDAP and ASPA participating.

ASPA SNAPSHOT

- ASPA establishes a Professional Development Department.
- The World Federation of Personnel Management Associations (WFPMA) is formed.
- ASPA bylaws are amended to include the president of the ASPA Accreditation Institute (AAI) to be an automatic member of the Board.
- AAI holds its first exam in April. By year's end, 346 people have become accredited.
- ASPA publishes its first book, *Reference Checking*, to help HR professionals follow up on employee references.
- The Annual Conference is held in San Diego.
- Conference attendance: 1,826.
- Conference registration fees: $95 for members, $135 for nonmembers and $60 for students.
- Conference exhibitors: 81.
- Conference surplus: $76,413.
- Membership: 19,471.
- Committees: 27.
- Board members: 44.
- Annual budget: $716,000.
- Reserves: $281,819.

Leaders of ASPA saw that the time had come to establish a Professional Development Department to organize educational opportunities for members. ASPA seminars quickly earned a reputation for being the best in the business.

In January, Herbert G. Heneman, Ph.D., a professor at the University of Minnesota Industrial Relations Center and an ASPA Accreditation Institute board member, became the first person to apply for accredited status. Twenty-eight years earlier in 1948, he was a scholar who had already devoted himself to the emerging personnel profession and was calling for accreditation of the personnel executive. His foresight originally sparked the effort that culminated in the accreditation program.

In September, the Board approved the following policy statement on occupational safety and health:

Providing a safe and healthful work environment is a fundamental responsibility of management. In order for management to fulfill this responsibility, cooperation with safety and health programs is the obligation of each employee. The rights and responsibilities of management to effectively direct the operations of an enterprise should not be restricted or curtailed by governmental rules and regulations, so long as the goal of health and safety of workers is not jeopardized. The Occupational Safety and Health Act (OSH Act) presently imposes a greater degree of government control than is prudent to encourage voluntary compliance.

Any occupational safety and health law and its administrative policies and procedures should recognize its resulting economic impact upon the business community. To achieve this end, the law must give adequate and equitable recognition to effects which may differ depending upon company size, inherent differences among varying industries and level of capital assets, as well as the costs to be incurred and the benefits to be derived.

There should be provisions for due process to all parties and an effective separation of standard setting, enforcement and judicial functions under the law. In addition, recognizing that the key to effective implementation of the OSH Act is voluntary compliance, there should be provisions for effective consultative and educational services for employers. Such services should be provided without risk of penalty.

The motion was passed with one dissenting vote. A discussion then ensued about how to disseminate the policy statement; the idea to make the policy a press release was voted down, and it was agreed that the Society's Washington, D.C., representative be consulted before the policy was disseminated.

1977 WORLD EVENTS

- President Carter pardons Vietnam War draft evaders.
- The space shuttle Enterprise takes its maiden flight on top of a Boeing 747 at Edwards Air Force Base in California.
- *Star Wars* opens in movie theaters and subsequently becomes the highest-grossing film to date.
- Elvis Presley dies of a drug overdose.
- The World Health Organization announces the eradication of smallpox.
- Popular movies: *Close Encounters of the Third Kind, The Goodbye Girl, Saturday Night Fever, Star Wars.*

ASPA SNAPSHOT

❖ The ASPA Board agrees to amend the ASPA Accreditation Institute (AAI) bylaws to divest the ASPA Board of the responsibility to elect members of the AAI board and to allow AAI to elect its own board members.

❖ ASPA/I, or ASPA International, is formed and becomes the Society's first chapter for personal development of professionals who work for organizations with international interests.

❖ Dues for both domestic and international members are increased by $10. Dues will be $50 for domestic members and $40 for international members. The increase will become effective in 1978.

❖ The Relocation Committee recommends that ASPA headquarters be relocated to Washington, D.C. The Board votes down the recommendation, noting that it is satisfied with the representation the Society currently has in the Washington, D.C., office.

❖ Membership: 22,221 (19,416 professional members and 2,805 student members).

❖ Committees: 24.

- Popular songs: *Tonight's the Night, I Want to Be Your Everything, Best of My Love.*
- Popular TV shows: *60 Minutes, Little House on the Prairie, Eight Is Enough, The Love Boat.*
- Popular books: *The Silmarillion*, J.R.R. Tolkien and Christopher Tolkien; *The Thorn Birds*, Colleen McCullough; *Looking Out for #1*, Robert Ringer.
- Average annual U.S. family income: $16,010.

In 1977, the Board agreed to form ASPA/I, or ASPA International, based on the recommendation of ASPA Board member Bill Johnson.

Board treasurer John Blodger testified before the House Labor Management subcommittee on the Education and Labor Committee about labor law reform. Labor interests were lobbying hard for its passage. In a Society first, the Board agreed to participate in a coalition to fight the legislation and joined with the National Association of Manufacturers, the Chamber of Commerce and 350 other groups. That same year, Ronald C. Pilenzo, Ph.D., SPHR, and another ASPA member testified before the House Subcommittee on Social Security and, according to Board minutes, "were well-received." An ASPA position paper on Social Security was also presented to the Senate Finance Committee.

ASPA was also moving forward in achieving its affirmative action goals. Although it was decided that affirmative action goals would not be required of chapters, there were affirmative action goals for the headquarters staff and the Board.

Earlier in the year, a committee of the Board recommended relocating headquarters to Washington, D.C. "There was quite a bit of debate on moving to Washington, and some people felt very strongly about not moving," said 1977 ASPA President Rudolph Weber, SPHR. A motion to move the headquarters to Washington, D.C., passed by just one vote. "Debate was even continuing after the vote was taken. I told the group that in no way did we have a mandate to move, so I suggested that we table the proposal for future consideration."

1978 WORLD EVENTS

- The Personnel Reform Act passes both chambers of Congress.
- The first computer bulletin board system is created in Chicago.
- The tanker Amoco Cadiz splits in two off the coast of Brittany, France, and spills 50,000 metric tons of crude oil.
- In *University of California vs. Bakke*, the Supreme Court bars the quota system in college admissions but approves programs that give advantages to minorities.
- Vietnam attacks Cambodia.
- In Jonestown, Guyana, Jim Jones leads his Peoples Temple cult in a mass murder-suicide that claims 918 lives, including more than 270 children.
- Sony introduces the Walkman.
- Popular movies: *The Deer Hunter, Midnight Express, Heaven Can Wait.*
- Popular songs: *Shadow Dancing, Night Fever, You Light Up My Life.*
- Popular TV shows: *Taxi, Alice, WKRP in Cincinnati.*
- Popular books: *And Still I Rise*, Maya Angelou; *The World According to Garp*, John Irving; *War and Remembrance*, Herman Wouk.
- Average annual U.S. family income: $15,060.

In *University of California vs. Bakke*, the Supreme Court approved limiting affirmative action to ensure that no reverse discrimination could occur. Bakke, a white applicant, was rejected twice from the University of California, Davis, medical school, even though there were minority applicants admitted whose scores were significantly lower than his. In a close decision, the Court held that race could be one of the factors considered in choosing a diverse student body in university admissions decisions. The Court also held that the use of quotas in such affirmative action programs was not permissible (UC-Davis maintained a 16 percent minority quota). Bakke was admitted to the school.

In January 1978, the Society received a letter from the International Association of Personnel Women requesting that ASPA not go to Florida for a national conference or to any state not supporting the Equal Rights Amendment and that the Society not spend money in those states. After some discussion, the executive committee of the Board agreed that ASPA should not support an economic boycott of any national conference, workshop or seminar sponsored by ASPA that was already committed or that would be committed in the future.

1979 WORLD EVENTS

- Vietnam announces the fall of the Cambodian capital of Phnom Penh and the collapse of the Pol Pot regime.
- The shah flees Iran after a year of unrest in the country. Muslim leader Ayatollah Khomeini takes over.
- Margaret Thatcher becomes Britain's new prime minister.
- The U.S. and the People's Republic of China establish full diplomatic relations.
- Egypt's President Anwar Sadat and Israel's Prime Minister Menachem Begin sign a peace treaty.
- A nuclear power plant accident occurs at Three Mile Island in Pennsylvania, releasing radiation.

History of ASPA Accreditation Institute

In 1948, Herbert G. Heneman, Ph.D., a professor at the University of Minnesota, wrote an article on the value of certification that ultimately culminated in the creation of the ASPA Accreditation Institute. In 1973, ASPA formed a task force to investigate the possibility of creating a certification for the profession. Later that year, the Board approved the task force's recommendations, and seven committees were appointed to develop recommended criteria, outlines for tests and test questions. An agreement was made with the Psychological Corporation to administer and analyze the tests. In June 1975, the task force was dissolved and the ASPA Accreditation Institute (originally the PAIRA Institute) was organized. The first accreditation tests were administered to 80 test takers in April 1976, with 82 percent of the candidates passing the exam. The designations awarded were the Accredited Personnel Diplomat (APD), the Accredited Personnel Manager (APM) and the Accredited Executive in Personnel (AEP). In 1977, the ASPA Board agreed to disassociate its involvement with the accreditation process and the ASPA Accreditation Institute became a separate organization with its own board of directors.

- China becomes the first nation in the world to register a population of 1 billion people. The One Child Policy is implemented in China.
- The 1979 energy crisis occurs in the wake of the Iranian Revolution.
- Popular movies: *Apocalypse Now, All that Jazz, Kramer vs. Kramer.*
- Popular songs: *My Sharona, Bad Girls, Le Freak.*
- Popular TV shows: *That's Incredible!, Alice, Dallas.*

ASPA SNAPSHOT

- The dues increase approved in 1977 goes into effect.

- The Annual Conference hosts between 70 and 100 foreign delegates from Mexico, Korea, Germany and France, the largest international presence ever.

- The ASPA Foundation funds research in accounting, productivity, training aids, and an analysis of the consumer price index as compared to increased wages and fringe benefits.

- Membership tops 20,000.

- Chapters: nearly 300.

ASPA SNAPSHOT

- John Blodger becomes the first African-American president of ASPA.

- Ronald Pilenzo, a long-time ASPA member, is selected to succeed Leonard Brice as executive vice president, effective in 1980.

- The Board approves an annual dues increase from $50 to $60, effective in 1980.

- More than 3,000 people attend the Annual Conference.

- Membership: nearly 28,500.

- The ASPA Accreditation Institute changes its name to the Personnel Accreditation Institute (PAI).

- Popular books: *Offshore*, Penelope Fitzgerald; *The Dead Zone*, Stephen King; *Sophie's Choice*, William Styron.

- Average annual U.S. family income: $16,530.

With the pending retirement of Leonard Brice, the Board spent much of the year searching for a new executive director.

Ronald Pilenzo, a long-time volunteer leader and personnel director for International Multifoods Company in Minneapolis, was selected to succeed Leonard Brice, effective in 1980. When Pilenzo took over, he was given the title of president and chief operating officer to better reflect his role. At the same time, the head of the Board of Directors took the new title of chairman.

Pilenzo envisioned operating the Society according to a more corporate model. "Len Brice had his own style, which was a little loose and very informal and which benefited ASPA at the time," said Pilenzo in an article on the 50th anniversary of the Society. "But I thought that for ASPA to meet its potential that we had to run it like a corporation. Len understood this, too, and he knew it was time for him to retire and hand the job over to someone else."

ASPA continued to become more involved in government affairs. The Board minutes reflect that the Equal Employment Opportunity Commission's focus for the coming year would be on layoffs and job sharing, the handicapped, and job evaluations.

RECAP OF KEY EVENTS IN HUMAN RESOURCE MANAGEMENT

1970–1979

1971   The Occupational Safety and Health Act (OSH Act) goes into effect.

1973   ASPA celebrates its 25th anniversary.

1974   The Employee Retirement Income Security Act (ERISA) is enacted.

1975   The ASPA Accreditation Institute (now the HR Certification Institute) is established.
        Certifications (now PHR and SPHR) began the following year.

1976   The World Federation of Personnel Management Associations (WFPMA) is established,
        with ASPA a charter member.

1977   ASPA/I is formed as an ASPA chapter.

1978   The Pregnancy Discrimination Act is enacted.

1979   John Blodger, SPHR, becomes the first African-American president of ASPA; later, the
        position is changed to chairman.

1979   ASPA membership reaches 28,471.

Everything was big in the 1980s—hair, clothing (more outlandish than big, but big in its outlandishness), inflation, debt—and if it wasn't big, it was fast-moving. The short-lived DeLorean was introduced in 1981 and became legendary in the movie *Back to the Future*. Personal computers and cell phones were big, too, but quickly shrank in size, and video game technology blossomed (in the early 1980s, *Pac-Man* was the rage; by the end of the decade, *Mario Brothers* was the most popular video game).

Not everything that was big and fast was good, however. Big business became even bigger, and with it came multimillionaires. Concerns started to be raised about excessive executive compensation.

Baby boomers in their 20s and 30s went on a spending frenzy, and binge buying and credit became commonplace; author Tom Wolfe dubbed the baby boomers the "splurge generation." At the start of the decade, inflation was in the double digits and drugs were so prevalent that President Reagan declared war on them. On the brighter side, the same people who were spending big were giving big; in 1989, Americans gave $115 billion to charity.

ASPA SNAPSHOT

❖ The ASPA title of president is changed to chairman.

❖ ASPA and the American Compensation Association work together for a project on comparable worth to reduce discrimination.

❖ Ronald Pilenzo, Ph.D., SPHR, becomes the president and chief operating officer of the Society, effective July 21, 1980.

1980 WORLD EVENTS

- The U.S. breaks diplomatic ties with Iran following the taking of American hostages in November 1979.
- Ronald Reagan is elected president.
- In a miracle on ice, the U.S. Olympic hockey team beats the Soviet Union and wins the gold medal. The U.S. boycotts the Olympic Summer Games in Moscow because of the Soviet invasion of Afghanistan.
- Union membership stands at 15,273,000, or 20.6 percent of the workforce.
- Popular movies: *The Blues Brothers, Caddyshack, Coal Miner's Daughter.*
- Popular TV shows: *The Dukes of Hazzard, The Jeffersons, House Calls.*
- Popular books: *The Bourne Identity*, Robert Ludlum; *Rage of Angels*, Sidney Sheldon; *The Covenant*, James Michener.
- Average annual U.S. family income: $23,204.

In 1980, ASPA hired long-time Society member Ronald Pilenzo, Ph.D., SPHR, to become president and chief operating officer of the Society. Pilenzo would remain in that position throughout the 1980s. ASPA also established the Council on Legislation, Education and Research (CLEAR), a group that would help raise the Society's awareness on Capitol Hill and within the profession.

Chief Justice Warren Burger administers the oath of office to Ronald Reagan at the Capitol, Jan. 20, 1981. (AP Photo/Bob Daugherty)

ASPA SNAPSHOT

◈ The ASPA Council on Legislation, Education and Research (CLEAR) finances an amicus brief filed on behalf of Gunther in *County of Washington vs. Gunther*, a case on sex-based wage discrimination. CLEAR also funds the ASPA/American Payroll Association publication *Best Pay Salary Administration*.

◈ ASPA publishes *Legal Analysis of Uniform Guidelines*.

◈ ASPA commissions a relocation study.

◈ ASPA has 241 international members in 37 countries.

Ronald Pilenzo, Ph.D., SPHR, becomes the president and chief operating officer of the Society, effective July 21, 1980.

1981 WORLD EVENTS

- Iran frees 52 hostages held in Tehran since 1979.
- President Reagan is wounded by a gunman.
- Sandra Day O'Connor is nominated as the first woman on the U.S. Supreme Court.
- President Reagan fires air-traffic controllers who go on strike seeking better working conditions and better pay.
- MTV goes on the air.
- Popular movies: *Raiders of the Lost Ark, Chariots of Fire, On Golden Pond.*
- Popular songs: *The Tide is High, Celebration, 9 to 5.*
- Popular TV shows: *Dallas, Alice, One Day at a Time.*
- Median annual U.S. household income: $19,074.

In 1981, ASPA's CLEAR funded an amicus brief and two publications, one a joint effort with the American Payroll Association and one on uniform guidelines.

The Personnel Administrator articles that year included "The Comparable Worth Issue," "A Reappraisal of Leadership Theory and Training" and "HRD: Promise or Platitude?"

1982 WORLD EVENTS

- AT&T breaks up.
- The Equal Rights Amendment falls short of the 38 states needed to ratify it.
- The Vietnam War Memorial is dedicated in Washington, D.C.
- Alexander Haig resigns as U.S. secretary of state.

- Michael Jackson's *Thriller* album is released and becomes the biggest-selling album to date.
- Popular movies: *E.T., Tootsie, Gandhi.*
- Popular songs: *Physical, Eye of the Tiger, I Love Rock N' Roll.*
- Popular TV shows: *One Day at a Time, The Fall Guy, The A-Team.*
- Popular books: *Schindler's List*, Thomas Keneally; *The Color Purple*, Alice Walker; *The Prodigal Daughter*, Jeffrey Archer.
- Median annual U.S. household income: $23,430.

The issue of relocating ASPA headquarters that had been tabled in 1977 resurfaced again. Ronald Pilenzo, now president and chief operating officer, had been on the Board in 1977 and understood the issue well. "This time we decided to do it right and study the situation," said Pilenzo. "So we hired a consultant, Jerry McManus, to assess our options. Now Jerry was completely independent of ASPA, so we were ensured that he would be objective about the decision." McManus recommended moving ASPA to either Atlanta, Cleveland, Phoenix or Washington, D.C. The Board narrowed the options to Cleveland or Washington. In the end, Washington was selected because of the available talent pool, national influence and, surprisingly, its affordability. It turned out that in terms of office costs per square foot, Cleveland was only slightly cheaper than Washington. ASPA leased space at 606 North Washington Street in Alexandria, Va., just across the Potomac River from Washington. ASPA eventually purchased the building, which would remain the Society's home until 1997.

ASPA SNAPSHOT

- ✧ The Board votes to relocate headquarters to the Washington, D.C., area. The location is later narrowed to Alexandria, Va.

- ✧ The Personnel Accreditation Institute (now the HR Certification Institute) develops new accreditations for senior specialists and senior generalists.

- ✧ ASPA goes on record opposing the Simpson-Mazzoli bill, which would legalize non-resident aliens and require a universal labor card for all workers.

- ✧ Dues increase to $75 for regular and associate members.

ASPA SNAPSHOT

- ✧ Membership retention rate is reported at 80 percent.

- ✧ The first ASPA Employment Law and Legislative Conference is held in March in Washington, D.C.

- ✧ The Board agrees to increase regular and associate member dues to $95, effective in 1984.

- ✧ ASPA's Council on Legislation, Education and Research is dissolved, and funds are returned to the ASPA general fund.

1983 WORLD EVENTS

- A Nation at Risk is published on the state of the country's education system.

- Sally K. Ride becomes the first female astronaut in space as a crew member aboard the space shuttle Challenger.

- A South Korean Boeing 747 jetliner bound for Seoul strays into Soviet airspace and is shot down. All 269 onboard are killed, including 61 Americans.

- A terrorist explosion kills 237 U.S. marines in Beirut.

- Vanessa Williams becomes the first African-American to be crowned Miss America.

- Popular movies: The Big Chill, Terms of Endearment, The Right Stuff.

- Popular songs: Every Breath You Take, Billie Jean, Flashdance… What a Feelin'.

- Popular books: Mistral's Daughter, Judith Krantz; The Little Drummer Girl; John le Carré; The Return of the Jedi, Joan Vinge.

- Median annual U.S. household income: $24,580.

Although ASPA's Council on Legislation, Education and Research was dissolved in 1983, the Society was still intent on establishing a public policy presence in Washington, D.C. The Society's first Employment Law and Legislative Conference was held that year in Washington, D.C., a conference that is still held annually. The conference would eventually allow time for attendees to meet with their lawmakers on Capitol Hill about key legislative issues of the day. This grass-roots initiative, originally voluntary, would later become the Society's HRVoice program.

The Society was also working to create a unified message on particular legislative matters. In September, the Board approved the following principle statement on employee and labor relations:

Employee and Labor Relations

Approved September 1983

ASPA Professional Principle Statement

ASPA believes that employers have the right to actively maintain direct relationships with their employees.

ASPA believes that employees have a legal right to have representatives of their own choosing consistent with applicable law.

ASPA further believes that state and federal legislation, administrative rulings and court decisions should protect the rights of all parties.

Our national economy, productivity and quality of work life are dependent upon the mutual understanding and effort of business, labor and government to develop constructive approaches to the allocation of resources and to the resolution of differences.

The balance between employers' basic freedom to make decisions within an organization and the rights of employees to be protected from illegal action must be preserved in the interest of both.

Increased productivity is dependent upon the maximum utilization of human resources.

Open, honest communication is a key strategy of effective employee and labor relations. Actions to interfere with the communication process shall be avoided.

ASPA also passed a health care cost management position statement encouraging employers to provide health care benefits.

ASPA SNAPSHOT

- ASPA moves from Berea, Ohio, to Alexandria, Va.

- ASPA publishes *Work in the 21st Century* and receives an Association Trends award for it. The book is published in 1984 but is written to commemorate ASPA's 35th anniversary.

- ASPA holds its first Leadership Conference in November.

- ASPA publishes *Fear of Firing—A Legal and Personnel Analysis of the Employment at Will*. The book is published in conjunction with the ASPA Foundation and is mailed to all members.

- Membership: 37,328 (33,800 professional members and 3,528 student members).

- Staff: 43.

- Reserves: $2.6 million.

1984 WORLD EVENTS

- Indian Prime Minister Indira Gandhi is assassinated.

- Geraldine Ferraro is the first woman to be nominated as a vice presidential candidate by the Democratic Party.

- The first Apple Macintosh computer goes on sale.

- President Reagan is re-elected.

- The AIDS virus is discovered.

- Band Aid releases the song *Do They Know It's Christmas?* Proceeds are to help in Ethiopian famine relief.

- Union membership represents 15.5 percent of the U.S. workforce.

- The U.S. Census Bureau estimates that there are 440,000 people engaged in HR work in the United States.

- Popular movies: *Ghost Busters, Indiana Jones and the Temple of Doom, The Karate Kid.*

- Popular songs: *When Doves Cry, What's Love Got to Do with It, Say Say Say.*

- Popular TV shows: *Family Ties; Murder, She Wrote; Cheers.*

- Popular books: *First Among Equals*, Jeffrey Archer; *The Fourth Protocol*, Frederick Forsyth; *Full Circle*, Danielle Steel.

- Median annual U.S. household income: $22,420.

There were probably a few ASPA volunteers who didn't get a chance to see *Family Ties* and *Murder, She Wrote* in 1984 because they were too busy engineering ASPA's move from Berea, Ohio, to Alexandria, Va. Staff who made the move to Alexandria included ASPA President and COO Ronald Pilenzo, Executive Vice President John Strandquist, Chief Financial Officer Jerry Hay and Jim Wilkins, SPHR, who held several positions during his long tenure at the Society. These dedicated staff members ensured the Society's continued operations during a time of extreme change.

ASPA's volunteer structure had always been vital to the workings of the Society. It wasn't until 1984, however, that the first Leadership Conference was held to bring together volunteer leaders from all levels of the Society. For the first time, volunteer leaders throughout the country could meet and learn about effective volunteer management practices and Society goals and initiatives. It also gave them an opportunity to network. This conference has grown significantly over the years and remains a much-valued event for Society volunteers.

The Society's commitment to public policy involvement was reinforced in the January issue of *The Personnel Administrator*. The cover featured this quote from ASPA Chairman James Skaggs: "If we must single out one priority, it would be legislation affecting productivity. We must also work toward breaking down the adversary relationship between labor and management."

1985 WORLD EVENTS

- President Reagan and Soviet leader Mikhail Gorbachev meet for the first time in Geneva.

- Two Shi'ite Muslim gunmen hijack a TWA flight with 133 onboard, 104 of whom are American.

- PLO terrorists attack the Italian cruise ship Achille Lauro.

- Terrorists hijack a Boeing 737 after takeoff from Athens. Fifty-nine people are dead as Egyptian forces storm the plane on Malta.

- Not to be outdone by their British and Irish cohorts, American artists form USA for Africa and record the song *We Are the World*.

- The Discovery Channel is launched by John Hendricks.

- Popular movies: *Kiss of the Spider Woman, Out of Africa, Prizzi's Honor, The Color Purple.*

ASPA SNAPSHOT

- Irene Florida, SPHR, becomes ASPA's Board chair. She is the first woman to serve in this position.

- A merger agreement between the ASPA Foundation and ASPA is signed.

- Based on a recommendation from the Strategic Directions Implementation Committee, the ASPA Board composition is changed. The Board will now consist of 15 people: the chair, vice chair, immediate past chair, secretary, treasurer, vice president of committees, six national vice presidents and three directors-at-large.

- The same report recommends the formation of state councils for each state and for Korea, Guam, British Columbia, Mexico, Puerto Rico and Bermuda. The report also recommends that all ASPA leaders, including chapter presidents, state council members, area board members and national board members, be ASPA members.

- The ASPA Foundation publishes *Sex and Salary,* a monograph on comparable worth.

- Committees: 9.

- Popular songs: *Careless Whisper, Like a Virgin, Wake Me Up Before You Go-Go.*

- Popular TV shows: *The Cosby Show, The Golden Girls, Miami Vice.*

- Popular books: *The Sicilian,* Mario Puzo; *If Tomorrow Comes,* Sidney Sheldon; *The Cider House Rules,* John Irving.

- Median annual U.S. household income: $23,620.

After nearly 40 years, the Society welcomed its first female chair in 1985: Irene Florida, SPHR. Under her leadership, the Society focused on taking the Board in a more strategic direction and honing the volunteer leadership structure.

The Board had formed a Strategic Directions Implementation Committee to oversee the process. The committee ultimately recommended a reduction in the number of Board members, the formation of a state council system and a requirement that ASPA leaders (including chapter presidents) be ASPA members. The recommendations also included the creation of standing Board committees (personnel, nominating, bylaws, and finance and strategic planning). The functional committees were public affairs; equal employment opportunity; compensation and benefits; employment and labor relations; employment and placement; personnel research; training and development; and occupational health, safety and security.

1986 WORLD EVENTS

- The space shuttle Challenger disintegrates 73 seconds after launch, killing all seven people onboard, including schoolteacher Christa McAuliffe.

- In "Hands Across America," 5 million people form a human chain from New York City to Long Beach, Calif., to raise money to fight hunger and homelessness.

- Austrian President Kurt Waldheim is discovered to have served as a Nazi army officer.

- A major nuclear accident at the Soviet Union's Chernobyl alarms the world.

- Popular movies: *Platoon, Hannah and Her Sisters, The Color of Money.*

- Popular songs: *That's What Friends Are For; Say You, Say Me; I Miss You.*

- Popular TV shows: *Night Court, The Golden Girls, Growing Pains.*

- Popular books: *Lie Down with Lions,* Ken Follett; *The Bourne Supremacy,* Robert Ludlum; *A Perfect Spy,* John le Carré.

- Median annual U.S. household income: $25,990.

This was a busy year for the nation and the profession, particularly in the legal and legislative arenas. In *Meritor Savings Bank vs. Vinson,* the Supreme Court ruled that sexual harassment is a form of illegal job discrimination. On May 19, in *Wygant vs. Jackson Board of Education,* the Supreme Court ruled against a school board's policy of protecting minority employees by laying off nonminority teachers first, even though the nonminority employees had seniority. In January, the Pension and Welfare Benefits Administration was established. The Immigration Reform and Control Act was enacted in November. The Age Discrimination in Employment Act was strengthened, eliminating the upper age limit of 70. The Tax Reform Act included provisions to simplify employer pension plan administration. The Consolidated Omnibus Budget Reconciliation Act (COBRA) was enacted, requiring that employers who provide health care benefits continue the

The Board votes to relocate headquarters to the Washington, D.C., area. The location is later narrowed to Alexandria, Va.

ASPA SNAPSHOT

❖ Area boards are established.

❖ The Board agrees to change the membership categories to professional (from regular), general and associate levels.

❖ Annual dues are increased to $135 from $95, effective in 1987.

❖ The Board votes to require newly affiliating chapters to have at least half, but not less than 10, of its members be ASPA members. The Board also votes to require that chapter presidents be ASPA members.

❖ Board members: More than 40.

benefits to formerly covered individuals for a period of time after employer coverage ends.

1987 WORLD EVENTS

- British Prime Minister Margaret Thatcher wins a third term.
- Klaus Barbie, a Gestapo wartime chief, is sentenced to life by a French court for war crimes.
- The Supreme Court rules that Rotary Clubs must admit women.
- The Iran-Contra scandal continues. Oliver North testifies before Congress that higher officials approved his secret operations, and John Poindexter, former national security advisor, testifies that he authorized the use of Iran arms sales to aid the Contras.
- The stock market crashes on October 19, Black Monday.
- Popular movies: *Moonstruck, Wall Street, The Last Emperor.*
- Popular songs: *Walk Like an Egyptian, Alone, The Way It Is.*
- Popular TV shows: *Highway to Heaven, Newhart, Growing Pains.*
- Popular books: *The Eyes of the Dragon,* Stephen King; *Windmills of the Gods,* Sidney Sheldon; *Presumed Innocent,* Scott Turow.
- Median annual U.S. household income: $25,990.

On February 25, in *United States vs. Paradise,* the Supreme Court ordered specific racial quotas to correct Alabama's persistent resistance to reforming its hiring practices. In 1970, a federal court had ordered the state to reform its hiring practices to end "pervasive, systematic and obstinate discriminatory exclusion of blacks." Twelve years later, the state still had not complied with the ruling. In response, the Supreme Court ordered the quotas, even though the use of quotas was challenged. The Court upheld the use of strict quotas in this case as one of the only means of combating the state's overt and defiant racism.

Susan R. Meisinger, SPHR, joined the Society in 1987 as vice president of government affairs. She had served as deputy undersecretary for the Department of Labor and knew the Washington political scene well. Under her leadership, the Society's influence on Capitol Hill grew quickly.

In September, ASPA published *Worklife Visions,* written by Jeffrey Hallett. The book was written for the workforce of 2007 and represented more than a decade of study on the issues of change, productivity, personal growth and HR management.

1988 WORLD EVENTS

- The U.S. and Canada reach a fair trade agreement.
- The U.S. Navy shoots down an Iranian airliner, mistaking it for a jet fighter; 290 people are killed.
- Pan Am flight 747 explodes from a terrorist bomb over Lockerbie, Scotland. All 259 people onboard and 11 on the ground are killed.
- Benazir Bhutto becomes the first Islamic female prime minister of Pakistan.
- Mikhail Gorbachev is named Soviet president.
- The Civil Rights Restoration Act is passed. The Act expands nondiscrimination laws to private organizations receiving federal funds.
- The Employee Polygraph Protection Act is passed.
- The Worker Adjustment and Retraining Notification (WARN) Act is enacted.
- Union membership represents 12.9 percent of the workforce.
- Popular movies: *Rain Man, Mississippi Burning, Bull Durham.*
- Popular songs: *Faith, Need You Tonight, Got My Mind Set on You.*
- Popular TV shows: *Roseanne, The Wonder Years, A Different World.*

ASPA SNAPSHOT

- Susan R. Meisinger, SPHR, is appointed vice president of government affairs for the Society.

- The Personnel Accreditation Institute changes its designations. They will now be known as the Professional in Human Resources (PHR) and the Senior Professional in Human Resources (SPHR).

- The ASPA Board agrees to develop the Learning System with Golle and Holmes Custom Education.

- *Worklife Visions* by Jeffrey Hallett is published in September.

- The Board is reduced to 15, with a goal to operate as a more strategic, corporate model.

SHRM SNAPSHOT

- The Board approves a name change to reflect ASPA's growing international presence and the profession's evolution from being primarily an administrative function to becoming a strategic partner.

- ASPA celebrates its 40th anniversary.

- The goal of 40,000 members for the 40th year is achieved.

- The Board approves a dues increase to $145, effective January 1, 1989.

- The Board approves a new mission statement.

- Popular books: *The Bonfire of the Vanities*, Tom Wolfe; *The Icarus Agenda*, Robert Ludlum; *Alaska*, James Michener.
- Median annual U.S. household income: $28,537.

As ASPA approached its 40th anniversary, there was increasing discussion on the need to update the Society's name. There had been attempts to rename ASPA during the 1960s and early 1970s, but the Board had rejected the proposals each time. "Frankly, the American Society for Personnel Administration just didn't describe us adequately anymore, and the name seemed very dated to us," said Wanda Lee, SPHR, 1990 Board chair. "Human resource management was the term everyone was using, so we thought why not incorporate it into our name?" The Board approved the name change this time, and in 1989 officially became the Society for Human Resource Management.

ASPA Board minutes were increasingly focused less on housekeeping items and more on strategic planning and government affairs. For example, during the January Board meeting, it was noted that HR had become a strategic partner in corporate America—the first time the term "strategic partner" appeared in ASPA Board minutes. In addition, during that same meeting, the Board discussed child care and mandated leave and agreed to take a legislative position opposing any proposal that would impose mandated leave.

In June, the Board approved a new mission statement for the Society:

To become the recognized world leader in human resource management by:

- Providing high-quality, dynamic and responsible services and products to our members/customers;

- Becoming the voice of the profession on HRM [human resource management] issues to business, government and the media;

- Establishing, monitoring and updating standards for the profession.

1989 WORLD EVENTS

- Tens of thousands of Chinese students rally for democracy in Beijing's Tiananmen Square. A nationwide crackdown on demonstrators occurs, and thousands are killed.
- The Berlin Wall is opened to the West after 28 years.
- Exxon oil tanker Valdez ruptures, sending 11 million gallons of crude oil into Alaska's Prince William Sound.
- Colin R. Powell is named the first African-American chairman of the joint chiefs of staff.
- A San Francisco earthquake measuring 7.1 in magnitude kills 67 and injures more than 3,000 people. More than 100,000 buildings are damaged or destroyed.
- Popular movies: *Glory, Born on the Fourth of July, My Left Foot.*
- Popular songs: *Look Away, Straight Up, Wind Beneath My Wings.*
- Popular TV shows: *America's Funniest Home Videos, The Wonder Years, Who's the Boss?*
- Popular books: *Midnight*, Dean Koontz; *Star*, Danielle Steel; *The Satanic Verses*, Salman Rushdie.
- Median annual U.S. household income: $28,910.

ASPA changes its name to the Society for Human Resource Management (SHRM).

SHRM SNAPSHOT

- In September, ASPA changes its name to the Society for Human Resource Management (SHRM).

- SHRM President and COO Ronald Pilenzo announces plans to retire in 1990.

- The Board agrees to the formation of a Human Resource Information Systems Committee.

- Section 89 of the Tax Reform Act of 1986, which would have required employers to test their benefit plans to make sure all levels of employees were treated fairly, is repealed. SHRM cites its members as integral to the Act's repeal.

- The Board considers establishing a political action committee. No action is taken.

- SHRM holds its first Global Conference.

- Membership: 48,388.

The Society had come a long way under Ronald Pilenzo's leadership. Membership had grown from 27,000 to more than 48,000, and the annual budget had increased from $3 million to more than $14 million. "I had been there 10 years, and it had been a great ride," said Pilenzo on his tenure as president and chief operating officer. "But I also felt that it was time for me to move on." Soon after the Society changed its name, Pilenzo announced that he would retire in 1990.

In 1989 Board minutes, issues surrounding the Society's name change prevail. Early in the year, two possible names—the Human Resource Management Society and the Society for Human Resource Professionals—were pitched to the Board. The Board was informed that both the names and trademarks were researched and that an audience search including CEOs, chief personnel officers, media and ASPA members was conducted on the names. A third alternative name was the Society for Human Resource Managers. The Board ultimately voted for the Human Resource Management Society and planned to send the proposed name change to ASPA members for approval.

That name would not come to be. During the March Board meeting, the Board was informed that the Human Resource Planning Society was challenging ASPA's potential name change and was threatening legal suit. In addition, the Board was informed that changing the name to the Human Resource Management Society would require ASPA to incorporate in a state other than Ohio.

A staff member proposed the Society for Human Resource Management (SHRM). That was the name that was put forth to members for approval. ASPA members approved it

by an 8-to-1 margin. ASPA would become SHRM, effective September 1, 1989.

Meanwhile, ASPA continued to work to meet its mission and vision. It went back into the seminar business in 1989. One of the major programs started that year was called "A Day With ..." It offered Society leaders and chapter members opportunities to meet and learn from prominent, nationally known human resource executives. The pilot program featured former ASPA President Robert Berra, SPHR, of Monsanto Company.

Besides the name change, Board minutes that year included discussion of Section 89 of the Tax Reform Act of 1986 (repealed later that year), which would have required employers to test their benefit plans to make sure all levels of employees were treated fairly; mandated benefits, particularly mandated leave; the quality of the workforce; Americans with disabilities; and child care.

A point/counterpoint story in *The Personnel Administrator* that year was "Can Unions Survive?" The magazine also featured articles on temporary assignments, employee recognition, older workers and how HR fits into the corporate picture.

RECAP OF KEY EVENTS IN HUMAN RESOURCE MANAGEMENT

1980–1989

1980   Ronald Pilenzo, Ph.D., SPHR, becomes ASPA's president and chief operating officer.

1983   ASPA holds its first Employment Law and Legislative Conference.

1984   ASPA moves its headquarters to Alexandria, Va.

1984   ASPA holds its first annual Leadership Conference.

1985   Irene Florida, SPHR, becomes the first female Board chair of ASPA.

1986   The Immigration Reform and Control Act (IRCA) is enacted.

1986   The Consolidated Omnibus Budget Reconciliation Act (COBRA) is enacted.

1987   *Workforce 2000* is published by the U.S. Department of Labor.

1988   The ASPA Learning System is introduced.

1988   The Employee Polygraph Protection Act is enacted.

1988   The Worker Adjustment and Retraining Notification (WARN) Act is enacted.

1989   ASPA changes its name to the Society for Human Resource Management (SHRM).

1989   SHRM holds its first annual Global Conference.

1989   SHRM membership reaches 48,388.

The 1990s were truly the technology decade. The World Wide Web was launched in 1991 (although some would argue that its origins go back as far as 1957) and changed people's lives. In 1993, 3 million people had access to the Internet. Just five years later, 100 million people would be online. E-mail changed how we communicated with family, friends and business colleagues. The idea of "24/7" access to work excited some but worried many.

It was an economically prosperous time, not just in the U.S. but in many other countries as well. The end of the Cold War led to demilitarization and political stability, allowing world leaders to focus on economic development, which led to higher standards of living. By the end of the decade, the U.S. unemployment rate was at just 4 percent and personal incomes had doubled from the 1990 recession.

It was a period of strong growth for SHRM as well, although it began on a rocky note. During the 1990 recession, SHRM lost members and closed 1990 $250,000 in the red. By the end of the decade, however, SHRM would exceed 130,000 members and have net assets equal to 91 percent of operating expenses.

1990 WORLD EVENTS

- The Soviet Union collapses when the Soviet Communist Party surrenders its power.
- The Hubble Space Telescope is launched.
- Microsoft releases Windows 3.0.
- The U.S. enters into a recession.
- The Americans with Disabilities Act (ADA) is enacted.
- Margaret Thatcher resigns as prime minister of the U.K. John Major succeeds her.
- The Channel Tunnel (or "Chunnel" as it was known during its construction) is completed when workers from the U.K. and France meet 40 meters beneath the English Channel seabed.
- Manuel Noriega surrenders power in Panama.
- The Gulf War begins.
- Popular movies: *Dances with Wolves, GoodFellas, Reversal of Fortune.*
- Popular songs: *Hold On, How Am I Supposed to Live Without You?, It Must Have Been Love.*
- Popular TV shows: *The Simpsons, Seinfeld, Murphy Brown.*
- Popular books: *The Bourne Ultimatum,* Robert Ludlum; *The Stand,* Stephen King; *The Burden of Proof,* Scott Turow.
- Median annual U.S. household income: $29,950.

President George Bush signs the Americans with Disabilities Act during a ceremony on the South Lawn of the White House July 26, 1990. Joining the president are Rev. Harold Wilke, rear left, Evan Kemp, chairman of the Equal Employment Opportunity Commission, left, Sandra Parrino, chairman of the National Council on Disability, and Justin Dart, chairman of The President's Council on Disabilities. Jefferson Memorial is in background. (AP Photo/Barry Thumma)

SHRM SNAPSHOT

- The SHRM Board agrees to raise member dues to $160, effective January 1, 1991. As of this writing, the dues remain at $160.

- The Board votes to make the president a CEO with voting rights on the Board. This will increase the Board to 16 members.

- Michael R. Losey, SPHR, becomes SHRM president and CEO, replacing Ronald Pilenzo, Ph.D., SPHR.

- The Personnel Accreditation Institute (PAI) changes its name to the Human Resource Certification Institute (HRCI). Celebrating its 15th year, HRCI's goal is to test 1,900 people in 1990.

- The face of SHRM members is changing. In 1990, 51 percent of all members and 40 percent of all volunteer leaders are women.

- SHRM develops a two-week residency seminar for HR executives at the University of Illinois.

- On January 1, *The Personnel Administrator* becomes *HR Magazine*; *Resource* becomes *HR News*, and *Who's Who in ASPA* becomes *Who's Who in HR.*

- Membership: 48,840.

- Chapters: 657 (437 professional chapters and 220 student chapters).

- Revenue: $13 million.

It was a busy year for the Society. Ronald Pilenzo, Ph.D., SPHR, retired after 10 years as president and chief operating officer. His legacy, however, went far beyond that; he was a long-time volunteer leader at the Board level before his appointment and was truly committed to both the HR profession and the Society.

Michael R. Losey, SPHR, became SHRM's president and CEO, effective October 15, 1990. "Losey's experience and expertise will be pivotal in guiding SHRM into the next century," said Wanda Lee, SPHR, chair of the Board at the time. Losey had nearly 30 years of experience in HR and was vice president of HR for the Unisys Corporation in Blue Bell, Pa. When Unisys was formed by the 1986 merger of Sperry Corporation and Burroughs Corporation, Losey played an integral role in establishing the organizational policy and operational framework for the new corporation. Before the merger, he had been with Sperry Corporation for 22 years.

It was a difficult year financially for the Society. By the end of the year, the Society's budget deficit was $252,000; the economic recession and an off-year financially for the conference took its toll.

However, as Pilenzo noted in a letter to the editor for *HR Magazine*, the Society was far from insolvent: "From 1980 to 1991 we had a surplus every year. In 1990 we missed our budgets because of the Annual Conference and the economic recession. Also, during these years we invested every penny we had in moving to Washington, D.C.; creating governmental affairs, meeting planning, membership, public relations, marketing and college relations functions; revamping the magazine; assuming responsibility for the Annual Conference from the chapters; investing in new computer systems; creating the Learning System; establishing the SHRM Foundation and the Accreditation Institute as subsidiaries and supporting them financially for years; reorganizing the governance structure; adding more than 100 chapters; and quadrupling the staff. If this is struggling, then I guess we were."

SHRM was moving ahead in establishing itself. That year, it co-sponsored a nationwide teleconference with PBS on employer compliance with the Drug Free Workplace Act. About 3,000 people attended the conference at sites around the country.

There was also growing involvement internationally. There were bilateral discussions with the French and British HR societies, a Far East trip was scheduled for early in 1990, and SHRM was planning a U.S.S.R. People to People Tour.

HR Magazine articles that year included "A Crack in the Glass Ceiling," "Diversity in the Workplace," "EAPs: Dawning of a New Age," "Soviets Seek U.S.-Style Training" and "All Managers Are HR Managers."

1991 WORLD EVENTS

- A cease-fire ends the Persian Gulf War. United Nations forces are victorious.

- Apartheid ends in South Africa.

- Boris Yeltsin becomes the first freely elected president of Russia.

- Armenia, Estonia, Latvia, Ukraine, Belarus, Moldova, Azerbaijan, Kyrgyzstan, Turkmenistan and Uzbekistan declare independence from the Soviet Union. The Soviet Union collapses.

SHRM SNAPSHOT

- Hilson Research legally challenges SHRM's logo. The Board agrees to defend the challenge.

- The Institute of International Human Resources is launched in June as a division of SHRM. SHRM members in good standing and with a responsibility for or interest in international human resource management can join the institute.

- SHRM appears on CNN for the first time. There are almost 500 media inquiries in 1991, a substantial leap from 300 in 1989.

- Major issues for the Society in 1991 include work and family, and education and training.

- The most critical priority for SHRM this year is the transfer of the strategic planning process from the Board to the staff.

- For the first time, the Human Resource Certification Institute (HRCI) does not require financial support from SHRM.

- Membership: 48,808.

- Clarence Thomas is nominated for the U.S. Supreme Court. Just days before the nomination goes to the Senate, sexual harassment allegations are made against Thomas. His nomination is confirmed but raises public awareness over sexual harassment issues across the country, in government and in corporate America.

- The Glass Ceiling Commission is created in November.

- President Bush signs the Civil Rights Act of 1991, strengthening civil rights laws and allowing damages in cases of intentional employment discrimination.

- Popular movies: *The Silence of the Lambs, Beauty and the Beast, Thelma & Louise.*

- Popular songs: *Rush Rush, (Everything I Do) I Do It for You, Baby Baby.*

- Popular TV shows: *Home Improvement, Designing Women, Coach.*

- Popular books: *The Kitchen God's Wife*, Amy Tan; *Cold Fire*, Dean Koontz; *The Secret Pilgrim*, John le Carré.

- Median annual U.S. household income: $30,136.

HR Magazine articles that year included "Automate the Entire Employment Function," "Making Room for the Whistleblower" and "Profiting from the Global Mindset."

For the first time in the Society's history, the strategic planning process was transferred to the staff rather than remaining with the Board, a sure sign of the Society's continued evolution as a nonprofit association and the Board's trust in the Society's leadership and staff. As the Society's program of work continued to expand, it became more important than ever to give the staff the ability to make key decisions between Board meetings. The time had come to end the practice of "managing over the transom," according to then SHRM President and CEO Michael Losey.

1992 WORLD EVENTS

- Four Los Angeles police officers are acquitted of beating Rodney King, an African-American. Riots erupt after videotapes of the police beating him are released.

- The Cold War officially ends.

- The U.S. lifts trade sanctions against China.

- The North American Free Trade Agreement (NAFTA) is signed.

- William Jefferson Clinton is elected president.

- The Socialist Federal Republic of Yugoslavia breaks up.

- A text-based Web browser is made available to the public, paving the way for millions of people to access the World Wide Web.

- Union membership stands at 9.7 million, or 11.5 percent of the workforce.

- Popular movies: *Unforgiven, The Crying Game, Glengarry Glen Ross.*

- Popular songs: *Save the Best for Last, Tears in Heaven, I'm Too Sexy.*

- Popular TV shows: *Northern Exposure, Picket Fences, 20/20.*

- Popular books: *Rising Sun*, Michael Crichton; *The Pelican Brief*, John Grisham; *Where is Joe Merchant?*, Jimmy Buffet.

- Median annual U.S. household income: $30,786.

It was time not just to meet SHRM members' information needs for today, but also to look toward what those information needs would be tomorrow. SHRM had periodically issued futuristic articles and books (such as *Worklife Visions* in 1987) but had not established a regular publication or program to follow and analyze workplace trends. It did so in 1992 with the publication of *Issues in HR*, which would later be renamed *Workplace Visions*. This bimonthly publication explores social, political, economic and demographic trends and how those trends may affect the workplace.

SHRM SNAPSHOT

The financial rough patch the Society experienced in 1990 seemed to have subsided. SHRM staff controlled expenses substantially that year and exceeded objectives by more than 50 percent. Other positive indicators included the success of the Employment Law and Legislative Conference, the growth of HR International (formerly ASPA International), the increase in the number of people taking certification exams and strong mailing list rentals.

The Society did not ignore pressing societal issues, however. Health care was becoming a nationally debated topic in the 1990s, and in response, the SHRM Board approved a set of health care principles to guide the Society. The principles:

- Any health care legislation should guarantee every citizen access to a basic core of health care services.

- Health care reforms should be based on a model that has built-in incentives to balance both quality and cost-efficiencies.

- The solution to the problem of the uninsured depends on the careful coordination and planning of all concerned parties. SHRM endorses the continuation of an employer-based system. The problem of the uninsured, however, is a societal problem and not a problem solely to be resolved by employers and other private payers.

1993 WORLD EVENTS

- President Clinton issues the "don't ask, don't tell" policy on the presence of homosexuals in the military.
- The Family and Medical Leave Act passes.
- The World Trade Center is bombed. A van bomb goes off in the parking area below the North Tower. Six people are killed, and more than 1,000 are injured.
- The Branch Davidian compound in Waco, Texas, is raided. A standoff begins. It ends 51 days later with a fire that kills 76 people.
- Popular movies: *Schindler's List, Six Degrees of Separation, Jurassic Park.*
- Popular songs: *I Will Always Love You, Freak, A Whole New World.*
- Popular TV shows: *Sisters, Frasier, Wings.*
- Popular books: *The Bridges of Madison County*, Robert James Waller; *The Client*, John Grisham; *Without Remorse*, Tom Clancy.
- Median annual U.S. household income: $31,241.

The SHRM Board continued to evolve, becoming more strategic in its orientation. In 1993, the Board issued the following position statement on sexual orientation in employment decisions:

SHRM strongly supports and appreciates the attributes and values of an increasingly diverse workforce. To that end, the Society welcomes supporting the concept of fair employment practices without regard to sexual orientation, with employment decisions being made on the basis of an individual's qualification, such as education, experience, demonstrated competence, and other attributes clearly related to effective job performance. Support for this concept is provided because of the Society's conviction that fair employment practices contribute significantly to the success of our membership and our members' organizations and to the competitiveness of our nation as a whole.

SHRM supports efforts which assist employers in adhering to this principle, but also preserve the employer's ability to select and implement employee benefit programs to support organizational objectives. SHRM opposes efforts which place additional costs and operationally burdensome

SHRM SNAPSHOT

❖ SHRM releases a new vision statement: SHRM: The Global Source for HR Professionalism and Leadership.

❖ The National Academy of Human Resources is formed.

❖ The Board approves health care principles.

❖ The SHRM Board establishes an internal Diversity Steering Committee and appoints a SHRM staff liaison to that committee.

❖ SHRM begins publishing *Issues in HR*, a bimonthly report on emerging workplace issues. Today, the publication is known as *Workplace Visions*.

❖ Membership: 53,209.

administrative demands on employers through mandated benefits, or which result in increased litigation or other organizational expenses that do nothing to encourage job creation and employment opportunities.

Taking this position was not without risk; SHRM received criticism from the public on this position and for its diversity initiative. Some people, it seemed, did not believe diversity to be an important component of the work of human resource professionals.

In June, the SHRM Diversity Initiative was formally announced at the SHRM Annual Conference. SHRM chapters were surveyed on their current or desired involvement in the area of diversity management, and a volunteer leader resource guide on diversity was distributed at the SHRM Leadership Conference in November. The initiative grew during the years, and SHRM created a brand name for itself as a leading organization in the diversity management field.

1994 WORLD EVENTS

- Rwandan genocide of Tutsis by Hutus begins; 800,000 people are killed in 100 days.

- South Africa holds its first interracial national election in April. Nelson Mandela is elected president.

- President Clinton is accused of sexual harassment while he was governor of Arkansas.

- A major earthquake hits Los Angeles, and 51 people die.

- O.J. Simpson's wife, Nicole Brown Smith, and her friend, Ron Goldman, are murdered. Simpson is accused of the murder, tried and found not guilty.

- Major-league baseball players strike, and the World Series is canceled.

- The Uniformed Services Employment and Reemployment Rights Act (USERRA) is enacted.

- Popular movies: *Forrest Gump, Pulp Fiction, The Shawshank Redemption.*

- Popular songs: *The Sign, I Swear, The Power of Love.*

- Popular TV shows: *E.R., Seinfeld, Friends.*

- Popular books: *The Celestine Prophecy*, James Redfield; *Disclosure*, Michael Crichton; *Remember Me*, Mary Higgins Clark.

- Median annual U.S. household income: $32,264.

Historically, the nonprofit sector has never had a reputation for acting quickly. SHRM broke this rule in 1994, though, when it launched an online forum on Prodigy and became one of the first associations to establish an online presence. Just eight months later, that forum was abandoned when SHRM established SHRM Online, www.shrm.org. SHRM President and CEO Michael Losey attributes the success of the early launch to the Board's move toward becoming more strategic. "We didn't have to wait for the next Board meeting or the meeting after that to make a proposal to go online and then wait for the Board's decision. We knew it was the right thing to do, and we did it." SHRM Online has become one of the most popular member benefits offered by SHRM.

The Society's legislative activity continued in 1994. The Board adopted an umbrella Fair Employment Practices statement, which reaffirmed and incorporated existing fair employment practices statements on ethnicity, gender, disability, age, national origin, sexual orientation,

1990s

SHRM SNAPSHOT

- The SHRM Board adopts the SHRM Diversity Initiative plan developed by the Diversity Steering Committee. The Board directs SHRM staff to integrate the plan into the operating plan, with vice presidents taking major accountability for the achievement of the plan.

- The Board agrees to establish special interest groups (SIGs). SIGs later become known as PEGs (professional emphasis groups).

- The Board approves a position on sexual orientation in employment decisions.

- The Newspaper Personnel Relations Association becomes the Society's first PEG after 99 percent of NPRA members approve the idea.

- Conference attendance: 4,556.

- Membership: 58,759.

Michael R. Losey, SPHR, becomes SHRM president and CEO, replacing Ronald Pilenzo, Ph.D., SPHR.

appearance, genetic background and legal off-the-job activities. In addition, the Board approved a statement encouraging fair employment practices without regard to a person's appearance except when it is for bona fide business purposes. SHRM staff continued to monitor such legislative issues as striker replacement, Occupational Safety and Health Act reform, a proposed Medicare/Medicaid databank, health care reform and a Congressional Coverage bill that would require congressional staff to be covered by the same laws as those in the private sector.

HR Magazine articles that year included "Big Returns for Award Bucks," "Finding the Gold in the Graying of America" and "Fitting Square Pegs Into Round Holes."

1995 WORLD EVENTS

- On April 19, the Alfred P. Murrah Federal Building in Oklahoma City is bombed and 168 people are killed.

- The first legislation passed by the 104th Congress is the Congressional Accountability Act. SHRM initiated and strongly influenced passage by heading the Congressional Coverage Coalition.

- On July 19, in the White House guidelines on affirmative action, President Clinton calls for the elimination of any program that: 1) creates a quota, 2) creates preferences for unqualified individuals, 3) creates reverse discrimination, or 4) continues even after its equal opportunity purposes have been achieved.

- A nerve gas attack in the Tokyo subway system kills eight and injures thousands. The Aum Shinrikyo ("Supreme Truth") cult is held accountable.

- The Million Man March draws hundreds of thousands of African-American men to Washington, D.C.

- Yahoo! is founded.

- Popular movies: *Babe, Braveheart, The Usual Suspects.*

- Popular songs: *Gangsta's Paradise, Waterfalls, Creep.*

- Popular TV shows: *E.R., Boston Common, Frasier.*

- Popular books: *The Rainmaker*, John Grisham; *Beach Music*, Pat Conroy; *The Horse Whisperer*, Nicholas Evans.

- Median annual U.S. household income: $34,076.

As part of the launch of SHRM Online, SHRM offered a demonstration of the web site during the Annual Conference. Many conference attendees (and a few of their more technologically savvy children) enjoyed surfing the Web, an activity many had not experienced before.

SHRM's government affairs activities continued and were used (along with SHRM surveys) to increase the Society's visibility in the press. Press releases issued by SHRM that year: "Lack of Congressional Action Makes Tuition too Costly for Hardworking Americans," "SHRM Files Amicus Brief in Hearing on Administration's Striker Replacement Order," "Salary Survey Indicates Growing Involvement for HR in Strategic Planning and Customer Service" and "Reference Checking Leaves Employers in the Dark, SHRM Survey Says."

68

A History of Human Resources

HR Magazine articles included "HR Practices that Promote Entrepreneurship," "Learning Organizations Evolve in New Directions" and "Diversity Danger Zones."

SHRM also published the first issue of *Mosaics: SHRM Focuses on Workplace Diversity* that year. The publication was designed to complement SHRM's workplace diversity initiative.

Debate continued about affirmative action, and the Society testified on behalf of SHRM members on the Family and Medical Leave Act (FMLA). SHRM also started a coalition to seek technical corrections to the FMLA.

SHRM's mission statement in 1995:

Through the efforts of committed volunteers and an empowered staff, be a recognized world leader in human resource management by

• Providing high-value, high-quality, dynamic and responsive programs and services to our customers.

• Being the voice of the profession on workplace issues guiding the advancement of the human resource profession.

SHRM underwent a strategic review of the organization that year. The report explained that "protecting the traditions of the founders while skillfully anticipating the future is the basic justification for this exercise in strategic planning."

1996 WORLD EVENTS

- A ValuJet crashes in the Everglades, killing all 110 onboard.
- President Clinton raises the minimum wage to $4.75 per hour.
- President Clinton is re-elected.
- In March, in *Hopwood vs. University of Texas Law School*, the school's affirmative action program is challenged by four white law school applicants who say they were rejected because of unfair preferences toward less qualified minority applicants. The U.S. Court of Appeals suspends the university's affirmative action program and rules the *Bakke* decision invalid. In 1997, the Texas attorney general announces that all "Texas public universities [should] employ race-neutral criteria." (On June 23, 2003, the Supreme Court ruling in *Grutter v. Bollinger* invalidated *Hopwood*.)
- The Welfare Reform Act is enacted.
- President Clinton signs the Health Insurance Portability and Accountability Act (HIPAA), which is designed to provide portability of health insurance and increased privacy protections for individual medical information.
- Union membership represents just 10.2 percent of the workforce.
- Popular movies: *The English Patient, Jerry Maguire, Sling Blade.*
- Popular songs: *Macarena, One Sweet Day, Because You Loved Me.*
- Popular TV shows: *Suddenly Susan, Touched by an Angel, Law & Order.*
- Popular books: *Primary Colors*, Anonymous (Joe Klein); *Angela's Ashes*, Frank McCourt; *Cause of Death*, Patricia Cornwell.
- Median annual U.S. household income: $35,492.

SHRM SNAPSHOT

❖ SHRM launches SHRM Online, www.shrm.org.

❖ SHRM outgrows its headquarters building and seeks new offices to hold its expanding staff. The Board agrees to move forward with a "build to suit" option for a new headquarters facility. Later that year, the location is established and plans are drawn.

❖ The Board approves the establishment of the Consultants PEG, effective January 1, 1996.

❖ International members exceed 2,600.

❖ Membership: 71,320.

❖ Chapters: 429.

❖ Staff: 113.

❖ Revenue: $25 million.

Growth in Membership Since 1990	
2000	18.1%
1999	17.1%
1998	23.4%
1997	16.9%
1996	1.7%
1995	12%
1994	11%
1993	11.3%
1992	7.2%
1991	(0.9%)
1990	0.1%

In just a few years, SHRM had outgrown its headquarters building and construction was under way to build a second SHRM building on adjacent land. SHRM continued to become more active in government affairs and was a player in getting Congressional Coverage passed. This legislation ensured that congressional and White House staffers were covered by employment laws. That year, SHRM was also involved in lobbying for the repeal of the Medicare/Medicaid databank and passage of the TEAM Act. SHRM was also a player in the continued debate on health care and pension reform.

Several professional development programs were launched in 1996, including the SHRM Workplace Diversity Conference in conjunction with the National Diversity Conference and the Walt Disney World Approach to Human Resource Management.

The Board also approved SHRM President and CEO Michael Losey's proposal to form the North American Human Resource Management Association (NAHRMA). The coalition would include the United States, Mexico and Canada. The NAHRMA would be formally launched in April 1997.

HR Magazine articles that year included "HRIS Expenditure Justification," "In Search of a Successful Ethics Seminar" and "Lessons Learned in Skills-Based Pay."

1997 WORLD EVENTS

- President Clinton begins his second term.
- Hong Kong returns to Chinese rule.
- O.J. Simpson is found guilty of killing his wife, Nicole Brown Simpson, and her friend, Ron Goldman, in a civil suit.
- A U.S. Appeals Court upholds a California ban on affirmative action.
- The cloned sheep Dolly is "born."

- Madeleine Albright becomes the first female Secretary of State.
- The jobless rate is 4.8 percent in May, the lowest since 1973.
- The U.S. Census Bureau estimates that there are 590,000 personnel or HR individuals engaged in HR work in the United States.
- Popular movies: *As Good as It Gets, The Full Monty, Good Will Hunting.*
- Popular songs: *Candle in the Wind, Foolish Games, Un-Break My Heart.*
- Popular TV shows: *The Practice, Veronica's Closet, Just Shoot Me.*
- Popular books: *Cold Mountain*, Charles Frazier; *The Perfect Storm*, Sebastian Junger; *The Man Who Listens to Horses*, Monty Roberts.
- Median annual U.S. household income: $37,005.

For the first time in SHRM history, there were more at-large members joining the Society than there were members from the chapter network, possibly reflecting the effect of SHRM's Internet presence. Not only had SHRM Online been successful in meeting existing members' information needs; it was also extremely effective in attracting new members.

SHRM continued to evolve as an association, and in 1997 it adopted new vision and mission statements better reflecting its scope and depth:

- Vision: SHRM is the Global Voice of the Profession.

- Mission: The Mission of the Society for Human Resource Management is to Represent, Inform, Guide and Lead the Human Resource Profession into the 21st Century.

To meet that mission, a new strategic plan was launched; it included plans to create a global membership, increase legislative activity at the state level, form a new high-tech professional emphasis group, and implement new association management and financial software systems.

The Board reached one of its strategic goals almost immediately when later that year it approved a global membership category. Dues were set at $95. A global member had to be a member of an approved human resource management organization in the country in which the member resided, if such an organization existed.

HR Magazine articles that year also reflected the Society's mission to lead the profession into the next century. Articles included "HR Departments are Exploring the Internet," "The Great E-Mail Debate" and "Are You Ready for Virtual Teams?"

SHRM launches its web site.

SHRM SNAPSHOT

- ◆ Annual Conference has 6,209 registrants, with approximately 9,000 total attendees (including vendors) and 756 exhibit booths. The exhibit hall is the largest one to date.

- ◆ The new headquarters building begins being constructed at 1800 Duke Street in Alexandria, Va.

- ◆ Employment Management Association (EMA) members overwhelmingly approve the recommendation that EMA become a professional emphasis group (PEG) of the Society. The Board approves EMA as a SHRM PEG.

- ◆ Membership: 79,418.

1998 WORLD EVENTS

- President Clinton is accused in a White House sex scandal. He initially denies allegations that he had an affair with intern Monica Lewinsky but later admits to the affair. Later in the year, a federal judge in Arkansas throws out Paula Jones' sexual harassment case against the president. *The Starr Report* outlines a case for President Clinton's impeachment; he is impeached by the House but acquitted by the Senate in early 1999.

- Europeans agree on a single currency, the euro.

- Washington state becomes the second state to ban affirmative action programs (California was the first).

- The Worker Investment Act is passed.

- Union membership drops to 9.46 percent of the workforce.

- Popular movies: *Affliction, Elizabeth, Shakespeare in Love.*

- Popular songs: *Too Close, The Boy is Mine, You're Still the One.*

- Popular TV shows: *Ally McBeal, 3rd Rock from the Sun, Late Night with David Letterman.*

- Popular books: *Paradise*, Toni Morrison; *A Widow for One Year*, John Irving; *Tuesdays with Morrie*, Mitch Albom.

- Median annual U.S. household income: $38,885.

SHRM continued making a name for itself in Washington, D.C. In 1998, a position statement on religion in the workplace was approved by the Board. In addition, SHRM signed a formal Business Partner Enrollment Form to show its commitment to the Welfare to Work Partnership, a nonpartisan, nonprofit organization. SHRM also committed to a School-to-Work Summit to be held the Saturday before the Annual Conference.

In 1998, SHRM published *Future Focus: HR in the 21st Century* with Bruce Ellig, SPHR, former SHRM Board chair, and Maureen Minehan, then SHRM issues manager. The book looked at the future role of HR in relation to the role of business and government and employee resources in a changing world. Some conclusions: HR would be required to be more strategic, HR would be measured on business outcomes, HR must understand the learning needs of an organization in order to gain competitive advantage, and HR must more accurately anticipate an organization's strategic direction and operational effectiveness.

Since 1990, the Society had experienced incredible growth, not just in terms of members but also in its program of work. It was a continued challenge to manage that growth and to ensure that SHRM was meeting its members' needs. In 1990, membership grew just 0.1 percent, and in 1991 SHRM actually lost members. However, membership growth had steadily increased from 7.2 percent in 1992 to 23.4 percent in 1998.

1990s

SHRM SNAPSHOT

- SHRM moves into its new headquarters building.

- The Society's revenues exceed $38 million and result in an increase to net assets of $6.2 million.

- The North American Human Resource Management Association (NAHRMA) is launched in a signing ceremony at the SHRM Global Conference.

- The Board approves a new global membership category. Dues for global members are set at $95.

- Annual Conference attendance: 7,937.

- Membership: 92,677.

SHRM moves into its new headquarters building.

SHRM celebrated its 50th anniversary throughout the year and published a special 50th anniversary issue of *HR Magazine*. In addition to a history of the Society, articles included "Future Challenges and Opportunities for the HR Profession," "Future Focus: A Glimpse of What May Be" and an article by Michael Losey titled "HR Comes of Age."

1999 WORLD EVENTS

- The world is abuzz with dire warnings about the Y2K bug. None of the Armageddon-like warnings will come to pass.

- Two students open fire in Columbine High School in Littleton, Colo., killing 12 students and a teacher and then themselves.

- The number of Internet users worldwide reaches 150 million by the beginning of the year. More than half of those are from the United States.

- The first woman graduates from the Citadel.

- Popular movies: *Blair Witch Project, American Beauty, The Sixth Sense.*

- Popular songs: *Believe, Genie in a Bottle, Livin' La Vida Loca.*

- Popular TV shows: *Who Wants to Be a Millionaire, Dharma and Greg, Spin City.*

- Popular books: *Southern Cross,* Patricia Cornwell; *The Testament,* John Grisham; *Harry Potter and the Chamber of Secrets,* J.K. Rowling.

- Median annual U.S. household income: $40,816.

In 1999, SHRM published *Global Trends: Shaping the Workplace of Tomorrow* with Nathanial Semple, William Semple and Maureen Minehan. The book looked at the emerging issues and trends that were expected to directly or indirectly affect the relationship between HR management and the workplace during the next several years. Some issues that were raised:

- Moving to a knowledge economy.

- A diversified and aging U.S. workforce and using the skills of new immigrants.

- Workforce readiness.

- The devolution of public policy from the federal to the state level.

- Work/life balance issues.

- HR outsourcing, which would allow HR to be more strategic but which also may ultimately eliminate HR.

- Rapid changes in the workplace that would allow HR to reshape its role.

- The changing economies of third-world countries.

- The introduction of the euro and its effect on the U.S. economy.

- Cross-border corporate mergers.

- Communications and information technology that would require HR to be technologically agile and educated about the emerging market and regulatory trends.

- Managing the human enterprise in organizations all over the world.

SHRM SNAPSHOT

❖ SHRM celebrates its 50th anniversary.

❖ Membership in the Institute of International Human Resources (IIHR) is 3,804, Newspaper Personnel Relations Association (NPRA) membership is 640, Employment Management Association membership is 2,812, and the Consultants Forum (formerly the Consultants PEG) membership is 1,554.

❖ Michael Losey assumes the presidency of the World Federation of Personnel Management Associations in Caracas, Venezuela, in July.

❖ Membership: 113,335.

SHRM SNAPSHOT

❖ Susan Meisinger, SPHR, is named the Society's chief operating officer and is appointed to the Board.

❖ HR Magazine makes the Folio 500 list of the top 500 magazines in the United States, debuting at number 461.

❖ The Board begins discussions about expanding SHRM headquarters in Alexandria, Va. Later in the year, the Board approves the construction of a 78,000-square-foot building to be built behind the 1800 Duke Street building.

❖ SHRM's net assets equal 91 percent of operating expenses.

SHRM also published issue briefs that year, including "Language Policy in the United States" and "Medical Information: How Confidential?" That year's *Workplace Visions* focused on the future of health care, the growing need for elder care, the effect of technology on work/life balance, the global dispersal of employment resources, and the rise in home schooling and its future effects on the workplace.

Other SHRM goals included the creation of a research function within the Society, enhanced government affairs presence to extend SHRM's reach, more book-publishing activities, the development of an international certification program, the publication of information online in multiple languages and a centralized purchasing function. The Society also approved position statements on part-time work and the contingent workforce.

RECAP OF KEY EVENTS IN HUMAN RESOURCE MANAGEMENT

1990–1999

1990	The Americans with Disabilities Act (ADA) is enacted.
1990	Michael R. Losey, SPHR, becomes SHRM president and CEO.
1991	The Civil Rights Act of 1991 is enacted.
1992	The Institute for International Human Resources (IIHR) is created as a division of SHRM.
1993	The Family and Medical Leave Act (FMLA) is enacted.
1994	SHRM membership reaches 60,000.
1994	The Uniformed Services Employment and Reemployment Rights Act (USERRA) is enacted.
1995	SHRM launches its web site, www.shrm.org.
1996	SHRM holds its first annual Workplace Diversity Conference, now the SHRM Diversity Conference & Exposition.
1996	The Health Insurance Portability and Accountability Act (HIPAA) is enacted.
1997	SHRM holds its first annual Staffing Management Conference.
1997	The North American Human Resource Management Association (NAHRMA) is established.
1997	SHRM headquarters moves from North Washington Street to 1800 Duke Street in Alexandria, Va.
1998	SHRM celebrates its 50th anniversary.
1999	SHRM membership reaches 131,571.

chapter

2000s

seven

SHRM SNAPSHOT

- Michael Losey, SPHR, retires after a decade as president and CEO of SHRM.
- The Michael R. Losey HR Research Fund is formed and endowed with $1 million contributed by SHRM, the SHRM Foundation and the Human Resource Certification Institute (HRCI).
- Helen G. Drinan, SPHR, is selected to succeed Michael Losey as president and CEO of SHRM.
- The Board authorizes $3 million to accelerate SHRM's Internet presence as "the" site for HR-related issues throughout the world and for the public at large.
- HRCI tests more than 21,000 candidates.
- The SHRM Information Center responds to more than 60,000 inquiries.
- SHRM Online (www.shrm.org) has 800,000 monthly users; it contributes $3.7 million to net assets.
- Membership: 154,906 (representing a 217 percent increase since 1990).
- Chapters: 478.
- Revenue: $74.8 million.

2000 WORLD EVENTS

- Y2K fears do not materialize; many organizations had already modified their software, and few problems actually occur.
- The Internet stock boom ends.
- George W. Bush is elected president in the closest election in history.
- President Slobodan Milosevic resigns after widespread demonstrations throughout Serbia.
- Union membership drops to 8.99 percent of the workforce.
- Popular movies: *The Perfect Storm, Meet the Parents, Erin Brockovich.*
- Popular songs: *Breathe, Smooth, Say My Name.*
- Popular TV shows: *The West Wing, The Sopranos, Will & Grace.*
- Popular books: *Prodigal Summer*, Barbara Kingsolver; *The Last Precinct*, Patricia Cornwell; *The Rescue*, Nicholas Sparks.
- Median annual U.S. household income: $42,148.

In merely five years, the Internet had become a powerful part of SHRM. In a report to the Board in 2000, it was noted that 31 percent of new members came from the Internet. Sixty percent of SHRM members were now at-large, meaning they did not identify with any SHRM chapter affiliation. SHRM continued to seek ways to enhance its Internet presence. Starting in 2000, SHRM posted its survey results online for free and made them available for download.

There was continued concern about the profession's image. In Board minutes of that year, it was noted that while SHRM was well-respected, both HR and non-HR executives thought that the HR function needed to offer more to the organization in terms of strategic initiative; clearly, SHRM was helping move HR to the strategy table, but there was still a lot of work ahead.

The SHRM grass-roots program was restructured and renamed HRVoice; it became an educational member benefit for all SHRM members. The program provided regular legislative updates to all SHRM members and resulted in a 170 percent increase in the number of letters written to Congress on HR issues. SHRM's media requests also increased 45 percent over 1999, with more than 3,000 press inquiries.

SHRM established a Research Department that year, with the goal of developing relationships with the academic community and initiating a coordinated research function.

Dana Serony, left, and Sutton Giese work to remove nails from a piece of wood that was recovered from a demolished home in the Hurricane Katrina damaged area of the Lower 9th ward of New Orleans, Friday, March 21, 2008. Volunteers are spending their Easter holiday working to help the area recover from Hurricane Katrina which struck the area in 2005. (AP Photo/Bill Haber)

SHRM opens a second building at 330 John Carlyle, creating a SHRM campus.

SHRM SNAPSHOT

- SHRM opens a second building at 330 John Carlyle, creating a SHRM campus.
- The Board approves the new SHRM Code of Ethical and Professional Standards in Human Resource Management.
- The Society undergoes an extensive strategic review.
- SHRM charters its 500th chapter.
- Conference attendance: 11,405.
- Membership: 168,391.

Workplace Visions that year examined an aging America, the rise of free agents in the United States, the impending labor shortage, and globalization and the HR profession.

It was a good year for the Human Resource Certification Institute (HRCI) as well. The number of people taking the PHR and SPHR exams rose from 2,052 in 1990 to more than 21,000 in 2000. That year, HRCI would contribute $1 million to the SHRM Foundation.

SHRM was also working on new codes of ethics, this time, however, not just for members but for staff as well. In addition to the codes, SHRM would publish a toolkit for members.

Position papers and public policy statements issued by the Society covered topics such as comparable worth, total compensation and genetic testing.

SHRM Foundation funding resource areas were global HR, technology, HR measurement and the changing role of the HR profession. The foundation also funded a Towers Perrin book called *Making Mergers Work: the Strategic Importance of People.*

HR Magazine articles that year included "Corporate Universities," "Online and Overwhelmed" and "The Elder Care Gap."

2001 WORLD EVENTS

- On September 11, terrorists fly planes into the World Trade Center in New York City, bringing down Towers 1 and 2. Another plane flies into the Pentagon in Washington, D.C., and a final plane, also destined for Washington, crashes in a Pennsylvania field after the passengers revolt. More than 3,000 are killed.

- Enron, one of the world's largest energy companies, files for bankruptcy.
- Disaster recovery becomes a major issue for many organizations.
- Former Klansman Thomas Blanton is convicted of the 1963 murder of four African-American girls in Birmingham, Ala.
- The Office of the 21st Century Workforce is established by the Department of Labor in March.
- Popular movies: *Harry Potter and the Sorcerer's Stone, A Beautiful Mind, Ocean's 11.*
- Popular songs: *Fallin', Lady Marmalade, I'm Real.*
- Popular TV shows: *JAG, That '70s Show, Dawson's Creek.*
- Popular books: *The Bonesetter's Daughter*, Amy Tan; *John Adams*, David McCullough; *Death in Holy Orders*, P.D. James.
- Median annual U.S. household income: $42,228.

The Board decided in 2001 to hire an outside consultant to assess the Society's current position and future. Bain & Company was hired to perform the review, which focused on ensuring that SHRM understood and was meeting members' needs.

In the meantime, SHRM continued to meet its annual goals and objectives. The legislative agenda included pursuing technical corrections to the Family and Medical Leave Act, Fair Labor Standards Act reform, health care legislation, Fair Credit Reporting Act technical changes, the Americans with Disabilities Act, genetic discrimination and comparable worth. *Workplace Visions* that year examined privacy issues, Generation Y, diversity and the future of HR. And *HR Magazine* articles included "Strategizing for HR," "Making Telecommuting Work" and "Anatomy of an Employment Lawsuit."

SHRM SNAPSHOT

- Susan Meisinger, SPHR, becomes SHRM's new president and CEO.
- The Board approves a revised vision for SHRM: To serve the HR professional and advance the profession.
- *HR News* as a separate printed publication is discontinued. Content is moved to *HR Magazine* and SHRM Online.
- SHRM sponsors a PBS pilot series, *Back to the Floor*, and sponsors NPR's *Morning Edition*.
- An Ethics Advisory Council is formed.
- The mortgage for the Losey building is paid in full on December 30.
- The SHRM Information Center responds to 73,343 requests for information.
- SHRM launches SHRM e-Learning to provide online learning opportunities.
- SHRM delivers more than 226,000 professional development hours through conferences and seminars.
- Conference attendance: nearly 11,000.
- Membership: 174,038 (164,539 professional members and 9,498 student members).
- Revenues: $72 million.
- Increase to net assets: $4.9 million. SHRM assets now exceed $100 million.

2002 WORLD EVENTS

- Kenneth Lay, chairman of Enron, resigns. The company comes under investigation for hiding debt and misrepresenting earnings.
- Bush's "axis of evil" speech points to Iran, Iraq and North Korea.
- The international accounting firm Arthur Andersen is convicted of destroying documents relating to Enron. Arthur Andersen closes its doors.
- WorldCom, after admitting to misstating profits, files for bankruptcy, the largest claim in U.S. history.
- Tyco executives are indicted in a stock-fraud scheme.
- Former ImClone executive Sam Waksal pleads guilty to charges of fraud and perjury, among others.
- The Sarbanes-Oxley Act is passed in response to corporate scandals. The Act is wide-ranging and sets forth standards for all U.S. public company boards, management and public accounting firms.
- Union membership represents 8.61 percent of the workforce.
- Popular movies: *Lord of the Rings, My Big Fat Greek Wedding, Harry Potter and the Chamber of Secrets.*
- Popular songs: *A Thousand Miles, Get the Party Started, Complicated.*
- Popular TV shows: *24, CSI, Everybody Loves Raymond.*
- Popular books: *Atonement*, Ian McEwan; *The Lovely Bones*, Alice Sebold; *The Nanny Diaries*, Emma McLaughlin and Nicola Kraus.
- Median annual U.S. household income: $42,409.

Susan Meisinger, SPHR, became the Society's president and CEO in 2002. She was hardly new to SHRM, having joined the Society shortly after its move to Alexandria. Meisinger was well-known and liked by many SHRM members because of her extensive travels to chapters and state conferences. Under her leadership, the Society would experience even greater membership growth than in the 1990s, expand SHRM Online, and add offices in China and India.

But first, Meisinger had to address the results from various studies and reports being submitted to the Board. It made for an extremely busy year. The Bain & Company study, commissioned the year before, found that the major issues identified by SHRM members were: 1) staying current with HR issues, and 2) having access to HR-related information and professional development.

In addition, an Interim Governance Report recommended the following Board changes:

- The Board should reduce the number of directors over a period of five years to between 11 and 15 members.
- The Board should create a governance committee responsible for the overall design and composition of the Board, its processes and the manner in which it evaluates itself.
- The Board should modify the Board selection process so that Board members are recruited by the governance committee and that Board directors are recruited from the membership as well as from outside the membership and the profession.
- To build continuity, phase in three-year terms for directors within the next three years.
- The chair should serve a two-year term beginning in 2003.
- The president and CEO should become a nonvoting member of the Board and not be included in the total Board size.
- The COO position will no longer serve on the Board.

The volunteer leadership structure was also under review. In 2002, the HayGroup was hired to review the existing structure because of the changes to the Board structure,

New SHRM Vision Statement

SHRM serves the needs of the human resource management professional by providing the most essential and comprehensive set of resources available. In addition, the Society is committed to advancing the human resource profession and the capabilities of all human resource professionals to ensure that HR is an essential and effective partner in developing and executing organizational strategy.

Susan Meisinger, SPHR, becomes SHRM's new president and CEO.

alternations to SHRM's mission and vision, and the Society's rapid growth.

The HayGroup recommended that SHRM strengthen the role of and support to state councils and local chapters, foster the field networks to facilitate knowledge-sharing and best practices, and re-create advisory forums to the Board as the primary interface between volunteer leaders and the Board. The Board approved all of these recommendations.

In addition to conducting these reviews, SHRM launched its e-Learning program, was working on the SHRM Academy to be launched in 2003 and was working on identifying the education requirements for HR professionals. Legislative issues included phased retirement, targeted hiring tax credits, Fair Labor Standards Act reform (white-collar exemptions) and pensions.

The Board also approved seven strategic objectives for the Society to accomplish. These objectives were identified to either "Serve the Professional" (STP) or "Advance the Profession" (ATP).

STP:

1. Provide comprehensive information and tools to HR professionals to enable them to make informed decisions.

2. Help HR professionals develop their knowledge, skills and careers.

3. Be the recognized community for exchanging ideas, developing professional relationships and increasing HR knowledge.

ATP:

1. Set the agenda for the HR profession.

2. Ensure that HR is recognized for its contribution to business success.

3. Enhance the capability and credibility of the HR profession.

4. Build communities for the exchange of leading-edge business ideas and the development of professional relationships.

The Society's purpose as developed by its founders was to "advance and develop personnel ethics, methods and research toward higher standards of performance leading to the professional recognition of personnel administration." The Society's early years focused on providing HR-related information to personnel administrators who were starved of such information.

More than 50 years later, the founders' vision remained essentially the same. SHRM members still wanted information and professional development to make them better HR professionals. How that information and professional development were delivered today and in the future, though, was much different from what the founders could have dreamed.

2003 WORLD EVENTS

- The space shuttle Columbia explodes, killing all onboard. An investigation into the explosion cites egregious organizational problems at NASA.
- The war against Iraq begins.

SHRM SNAPSHOT

- SHRM is recognized as one of the "50 Great Places to Work" in the Washington, D.C., metropolitan area by *Washingtonian* magazine.

- Chairs now serve two-year terms.

- President Bush visits SHRM headquarters on February 12.

- A PEGs task force looks into the future of the PEGs, the cost of services compared to dollars received, the cost of staff support, PEG retention rates and the need to eliminate PEG boards.

- SHRM's media affairs staff field more than 2,700 media inquiries, leading to more than 4,800 articles in publications, including the *Wall Street Journal*, *The Washington Post*, *USA Today*, and the *Chicago Tribune*. Several articles feature the progression of HR into a strategic role.

- Membership: 179,994 (170,660 professional members and 9,334 student members).

- Professional chapters: 558.

- Revenue: $73 million.

- Operating expenses: $64.4 million.

- Increase to net assets: $9.6 million.

- The Supreme Court upholds the University of Michigan Law School's affirmative action policy, ruling that race can be one of many factors considered in university admissions.

- Saddam Hussein is captured.

- In *Nevada Department of Human Resource vs. Hibbs*, the Supreme Court rules that states can be sued in federal court for Family and Medical Leave Act violations.

- Popular movies: *Finding Nemo, Pirates of the Caribbean: The Curse of the Black Pearl, Bruce Almighty*.

- Popular songs: *Crazy in Love, Baby Boy, Miss Independent*.

- Popular TV shows: *Arrested Development, Buffy the Vampire Slayer, One Tree Hill*.

- Popular books: *The Da Vinci Code*, Dan Brown; *The Lake House*, James Patterson; *Bleachers*, John Grisham.

- Median annual U.S. household income: $43,318.

The SHRM volunteer leadership structure was still being refined in 2003, with the goal to change SHRM Board governance from constituency based to a strategic corporate model. The volunteer leadership structure was also being refined to reflect the Society's mission and vision and to reflect the Society's rapid growth.

In the end, seven regional councils were established, effective January 1, 2004, replacing the previous area board structure.

The membership requirement for newly affiliating chapters was also changed (effective January 1, 2004) from at least 10 of its members or 30 percent of its membership, whichever is greater, to 100 percent of its membership subject to a minimum of 25 members.

In 2003, SHRM developed and implemented a Member Satisfaction Index to track member satisfaction for three key audiences (new members, emerging members and most valued members). The intent of the index was to determine key drivers of satisfaction, the difference between member expectations and actual experiences, and member advocacy (word-of-mouth about SHRM) and loyalty; to understand the members' value proposition; to assess SHRM's strengths and weaknesses; and to determine why members join and renew.

SHRM had always had international members; ASPA history discusses international members from the time the Society was formed. In 1976, the first international chapter was formed; that same year, the World Federation of Personnel Management Associations (WFPMA) was founded.

As SHRM grew, international inquiries mounted. SHRM needed a strategic plan for its international activities. In 2003, the Board accepted task force recommendations for an international plan that refined the Society's international strategy. The task force recommendations included plans to:

- Market products, services and membership on an international level to targeted priority countries.

- Explore limited ventures in three countries chosen for their strategic importance: China, India and Canada.

- Implement a process to consider opportunities arising when potential international partners approach SHRM.

SHRM SNAPSHOT

- SHRM holds its first strategic HR conference.
- The Human Resource Certification Institute (HRCI) offers the Global Professional in Human Resources (GPHR) certification exam.
- SHRM eliminates the PEGs and creates virtual forums. The committee structure is also eliminated, and new panels of experts are created. The field structure is also streamlined, and more staff members are added to support the new structure.
- SHRM offers the Global Learning System.
- The SHRM/Rutgers LINE index is launched.
- SHRM publishes *2015: Scenarios for the Future of HR Management.*
- SHRM members send nearly 15,000 letters to Congress on various employment issues.
- Membership: 194,641.
- Member retention: 81.9 percent, the highest level since 2000.
- Chapters: 567.

In just a few years, SHRM would have staff and offices in China and India.

HR Week, a weekly e-mail to all members, was also successfully launched in 2003. SHRM Online was redesigned, and eight new online forums were launched to provide industry- and issue-specific information and networking to all members. SHRM added webcasts as a free member benefit.

SHRM also issued a health care position statement, engaged members in upcoming congressional and presidential elections, hosted executive roundtables with Dow Jones, launched the Best Small & Medium Companies to Work for in America program, expanded the SHRM Academy and designed a new conference on strategic HR.

Workplace Visions articles that year examined employer-sponsored pensions, mental health trends and disabilities in a technology-driven workplace.

HR Magazine articles included "From Workforce to Armed Forces—And Back," "Plastic Paychecks" and "Employer, Audit Thyself."

2004 WORLD EVENTS

- Former Enron CFO Andrew Fastow pleads guilty to defrauding Enron.
- The Abu Ghraib prison atrocities are brought to light.
- A tsunami devastates Asia. More than 225,000 are killed.
- Union membership falls to 7.92 percent of the workforce.
- The CIA admits that there was no imminent threat from weapons of mass destruction before the 2003 invasion of Iraq.

- Popular movies: *Shrek 2, Spider-Man 2, Meet the Fockers.*
- Popular songs: *This Love, Pieces of Me, If I Ain't Got You.*
- Popular TV shows: *House, Lost, Veronica Mars.*
- Popular books: *Angels & Demons*, Dan Brown; *My Life*, Bill Clinton; *Eats, Shoots & Leaves*, Lynne Truss.
- Median annual U.S. household income: $44,389.

SHRM's first strategic HR conference was held October 12-14, 2004, in Los Angeles. Additional strategic professional development opportunities were held in conjunction with the Wharton School of Business, Cornell University, the University of Southern California, Simmons College, the University of North Carolina-Chapel Hill, Manhattanville College and the Center for Creative Leadership. SHRM also sponsored events for chief HR officers of Fortune 100 Best Companies to Work For.

SHRM filed comments with various government agencies on such matters as the Uniformed Services Employment and Reemployment Rights Act, a proposed rule on Title II of the Americans with Disabilities Act and proposed standards for systemic compensation discrimination.

The SHRM Foundation created a new DVD called "Fueling the Talent Engine: Finding and Keeping High Performers."

Workplace Visions explored the effect of state-level public policy on HR. In addition, the *SHRM 2004–2005 Workplace Forecast: A Strategic Outlook* was published. Top trends identified included a rise in health care costs, a focus on domestic safety and security, and the use of technology to communicate with employees.

SHRM SNAPSHOT

- SHRM leases office space in Beijing.
- SHRM launches operations in India; Strategic Human Resource Management India Private Limited (SHRM-India) is incorporated on October 10, 2005, under The Companies Act, 1956, of India.
- The U.S. Chamber of Commerce recognizes SHRM as one of the 25 largest U.S. associations and one of the 100 fastest growing.
- SHRM sponsors the second annual 50 Best Small & Medium Companies to Work For in America awards.
- SHRM celebrates the 50th anniversary of *HR Magazine*.
- The Board approves an annual honorarium to all voting Board members, effective January 2006.
- Membership: 205,738.
- Professional chapters: 569.

SHRM opens offices in Mumbai, India, and also in Beijing, China.

HR Magazine articles included "Do Your Family-Friendly Programs Make Cents," "HR on the Board" and "Countering a Weight Crisis."

2005 WORLD EVENTS

- President Bush is sworn in for a second term.
- Iraqi elections take place.
- British Prime Minister Tony Blair wins his third successive term.
- London is hit by terrorist bombs, the worst attack there since World War II.
- Hurricane Katrina devastates the southern coast of the U.S., especially New Orleans. Americans are shaken by the severity of the storm and by the lack of preparation by the U.S. government.
- An earthquake in the Kashmir region of Pakistan kills more than 70,000 and leaves 4 million homeless.
- The Teamsters and Service Employees Union announces its withdrawal from the AFL-CIO, the worst union crisis since 1935. Days later, the United Food and Commercial Workers Union also withdraws.
- Popular movies: *Harry Potter and the Goblet of Fire, Wedding Crashers, Charlie and the Chocolate Factory.*
- Popular songs: *We Belong Together, Since U Been Gone, Because of You.*
- Popular TV shows: *Desperate Housewives, American Idol, Lost.*
- Popular books: *The Mermaid Chair,* Sue Monk Kidd; *A Breath of Snow and Ashes,* Diana Gabaldon; *The Closers,* Michael Connelly.
- Median annual U.S. household income: $46,326.

SHRM went global in 2005, leasing office space in Beijing and incorporating SHRM-India. The first SHRM professional development programs in India were held in late October.

HR public policy issues in 2005 included retirement security, corporate campaigns and employee representation rights, workplace safety, genetic discrimination, immigration, and health care. SHRM engaged in an organizationwide focus on health care, workforce readiness and offshoring/outsourcing issues.

Workplace Visions articles examined preventive health care, the future of retirement and the future of unions.

HR Magazine articles included "The Truth about the Coming Labor Shortage," "Demystifying Section 404" and "E-Learning Evolves."

In 2005, SHRM reached 121 million readers for targeted media. Total impressions for SHRM in the news media exceeded 600 million. SHRM staff also secured a regular column for the president and CEO in two European-based publications, *European CEO* and *Business Finance* magazine.

Membership Annual Growth	
1998	23.4%
1999	17.1%
2000	18.1%
2001	9.5%
2002	3.6%
2003	3.7%
2004	7.6%
2005	5.8%
2006	6.3%

SHRM Membership Between 1990 and 2007	
1990	48,840
1991	48,808
1992	53,209
1993	58,759
1994	64,826
1995	71,320
1996	79,418
1997	92,677
1998	113,335
1999	131,571
2000	154,906
2001	168,391
2002	174,038
2003	179,994
2004	194,641
2005	205,738
2006	217,242
2007	230,000+

SHRM's media reach also expanded when it sponsored CNBC's Executive Leadership Awards program, which included advertising and branding opportunities before, during and after the event on CNBC and in the *Wall Street Journal*.

Like so many other organizations, SHRM was also quick to respond to the Hurricane Katrina relief efforts. Led by the Member Services Division, efforts included enlisting volunteers for the American Red Cross, forging a partnership with the Employee Assistance Professionals Association and securing a 45-day reprieve on Form I-9 requirements. SHRM Online offered numerous resources and assistance in a special area. SHRM also extended membership for those in affected areas, granted funds to chapters and state councils for relief efforts, provided a Hurricane Response Employment Center, and offered direct and matching employee donations to the American Red Cross and Habitat for Humanity.

2006 WORLD EVENTS

- After weeks of student-led protests, France repeals a new labor law that would have made it easier for employers to fire workers under the age of 26.
- Iran announces that it successfully enriched uranium.
- North Korea explodes a nuclear device in the North Korean mountains.
- Saddam Hussein is convicted of war crimes against humanity and is hanged in Baghdad.
- Union membership falls to 7.4 percent of the U.S. workforce.
- Popular movies: *The Departed, Dreamgirls, Little Miss Sunshine.*
- Popular songs: *Bad Day, SOS, Temperature.*
- Popular TV shows: *The Office, Heroes, Battlestar Galactica.*

By all accounts, SHRM was successful: *HR Magazine* was named one of the top 10 business magazines in the United States in 2006, and the Society as a whole was named a "remarkable" association by the American Society of Association Executives and the Center for Association Leadership. SHRM continued to fulfill its mission to serve the professional and advance the profession.

In 2006, SHRM fielded a new human resource competency study to identify key competencies of HR professionals who add value to their organizations. The study was a joint effort between University of Michigan professors Wayne Brockbank and David Ulrich of the RBI Group.

SHRM also began offering programs for federal-sector HR professionals. At the Annual Conference that year, more than 50 chief human capital officers from various federal agencies attended a program called "Transformation Efforts on the Human Capital Front," featuring Harvard University professor David Gergen. In addition, SHRM held another program, "HR in the Public Sector: Meeting Critical Challenges," in collaboration with Harvard Business School Publishing.

SHRM's Executive HR Network held six regional events with Harvard Business School Publishing to give HR executives an opportunity to meet and network with each other. Partnerships also continued with the Wharton School of Business and the Disney Institute.

The SHRM Learning System also showed continued growth. In the past 14 years, it had grown from the three original college and university partners to a network of nearly 250 academic partnerships around the world.

SHRM SNAPSHOT

- SHRM Corporation is formed to assume activities of SHRM's online HR advertising program. SHRM Corporation will also serve as the registered agent in China.
- SHRM establishes the annual Human Capital Leadership Awards.
- The American Society of Association Executives and the Center for Association Leadership recognize SHRM as one of America's most outstanding associations in the book 7 *Measures of Success: What Remarkable Associations Do that Others Don't.*
- SHRM has members in 119 countries.

SHRM SNAPSHOT

- The Human Resource Certification Institute (HRCI) creates the California state HR certification.
- In June 2007, SHRM launches its refined brand and logo, which positions SHRM to: 1) remain the go-to resource for HR, 2) continue to attract and retain members, 3) be a career partner for success, and 4) champion the strategic role of HR.
- Membership: 236,000.
- Revenue: nearly $108 million.

The New American Workplace, funded by SHRM, was also published in 2006. It was co-authored by Edward E. Lawler III and James O'Toole of the University of Southern California.

SHRM offered is first joint event in Canada in conjunction with the Human Resources Professionals Association of Ontario. It was a SHRM Academy course, "Creating an HR Strategy for Organizational Success," and it was held in Toronto. At the same event, an additional invitation-only Executive Forum was held.

The SHRM Human Capital Leadership Awards were announced in October 2006 at the Society's strategic HR conference. The awards recognized excellence in four areas: strategic leadership, innovative business solutions, competitive workforce programs and human capital business leaders.

SHRM also unveiled the *SHRM Human Resource Curriculum Guidebook and Templates* to the academic community. The publication listed areas that all undergraduate and graduate students in HR management should study.

Workplace Visions examined productivity, global labor mobility, and women and work. The SHRM Research Department also published the *SHRM Special Expertise Panels 2006 Trends Report* and the *SHRM 2006 Symposium on Health Care Costs and the Future of U.S. Competitiveness.*

HR Magazine articles included "The Ethics Squeeze," "Diversity Finds Its Place" and "HR's New Role in Executive Pay."

SHRM continued its partnership with National Public Radio on "Marketplace Morning Report," a program that reached 13 million listeners each week. SHRM also helped develop and sponsor Marketplace's series "Conversations from the Corner Office," a monthly segment featuring successful CEOs who discuss leadership, business and people management strategies.

2007 WORLD EVENTS

- Nancy Pelosi becomes the first female speaker of the U.S. House of Representatives.
- 32 people are killed at Virginia Polytechnic Institute in Blacksburg.
- Tony Blair resigns as British prime minister.
- Tensions regarding the Iraq War escalate.
- Walter Reed Army Medical Center comes under criticism for its treatment of war veterans.
- Popular movies: *Spider-Man 3, Shrek the Third, Pirates of the Caribbean: At World's End.*
- Popular songs: *Hips Don't Lie, Over My Head, Big Girls Don't Cry.*
- Popular TV shows: *Private Practice, Mad Men, Pushing Daisies.*
- Popular books: *A Thousand Splendid Suns*, Khaled Hosseini; *The Almost Moon*, Alice Sebold; *Boom!*, Tom Brokaw.

The first state-level certification, the California certification (PHR-CA/SPHR-CA), was offered by the Human Resource Certification Institute (HRCI) in April 2007. It was designed to augment the PHR and SPHR certifications and to focus on knowledge of the laws and practices specific to California in cases where the laws are different from or need to be integrated with U.S. federal laws and practices.

SOCIETY FOR HUMAN
RESOURCE MANAGEMENT

SHRM releases new branding look in 2007.

Foundation
Investing in the Future of HR

CERTIFICATION
INSTITUTE
COMMIT TO A HIGHER STANDARD

SHRM Foundation and the HR Certification
Institute launch new brands in 2008.

The *2007–2008 Workplace Trends List* was published that year. The top trends identified, according to a special expertise panel, included the importance of globalization and integrating markets, the implication of rising health care costs, immigration and global labor mobility, the continuing skills shortage, and a greater reliance on metrics.

HR Magazine articles included "China: Land of Opportunity and Challenge," "Cultivating Female Leaders" and "Corporate Social Responsibility Pays Off."

Major legislative issues for 2007 included immigration reform, family and medical leave, health care, workplace flexibility, educational assistance, and gender discrimination.

2008 EVENTS

After 20 years at SHRM, Susan Meisinger announced her retirement as SHRM president and CEO.

Meisinger's contributions to the Society are almost too numerous to recount. Under her leadership as SHRM president and CEO, membership grew from 170,000 to 233,000 members, member retention increased from 79 percent to more than 81 percent, revenue increased from $70 million to more than $107 million, and reserves increased from $62 million to nearly $160 million.

During Meisinger's tenure, the Society truly went global, establishing offices in India and China and creating the Global Learning System. SHRM also launched a public affairs campaign to highlight the value of the HR profession; provided recognition for great HR practices; launched the 50 Best Small & Medium Companies to Work for in America awards and the Human Capital Leadership Awards; and began sponsorships on public radio, CNN, Fox, and the *CEO Exchange* on PBS.

In 2008, SHRM will work to retain 81.88 percent of its members and welcome 55,000 new members. It will expand and accelerate its initiatives in India and conduct a People to People program in China. Research will be conducted to determine the needs of the HR executive and how SHRM can provide information and services to attract this growing HR segment. In addition to executive roundtables for chief human resource officers, SHRM will hold its first-ever Diversity Practitioners' Summit, conduct a feasibility study for a SHRM university, continue its work on SHRM curriculum development and conduct a study on the state of HR education. And, of course, SHRM will continue to offer the largest annual HR conference in the world, publish *HR Magazine*, host numerous professional development opportunities online and throughout the world, produce top-notch research in the field, offer a continued presence on Capitol Hill and in many state legislatures, and host the premier online web site for HR information and job postings.

RECAP OF KEY EVENTS IN HUMAN RESOURCE MANAGEMENT

2000— Present

2001   Helen G. Drinan, SPHR, takes over as SHRM president and CEO.

2001   SHRM opens a second building in Alexandria, Va.

2002   The Board adopts a new dual mission to "Serve the Professional" and "Advance the Profession."

2002   Susan R. Meisinger, SPHR, becomes SHRM president and CEO.

2002   The Sarbanes-Oxley Act is enacted.

2004   The Human Resource Certification Institute (HRCI) creates the Global Professional in HR (GPHR) exam for global HR professionals.

2004   SHRM begins sponsoring the annual 50 Best Small & Medium Companies to Work for in America awards.

2005   SHRM membership reaches 200,000.

2005   SHRM creates the Strategic Human Resource Management India Private Limited in Mumbai.

2005   The U.S. Chamber of Commerce recognizes SHRM as one of 25 largest U.S. associations and one of the 100 fastest-growing.

2006   SHRM establishes the annual Human Capital Leadership Awards program.

2006   SHRM launches operations in Beijing.

2006   The American Society of Association Executives and the Center for Association Leadership recognize SHRM as one of America's most outstanding associations in the book *7 Measures of Success*.

2007   SHRM membership reaches 230,000.

2008   Susan Meisinger announces her retirement as SHRM president and CEO.

2008   SHRM celebrates its 60th anniversary.

There is no workplace Nostradamus who can predict with absolute certainty what the world and the workplace will look like 60 years from now, although it is probably safe to say that it will be significantly different from what we have seen before.

In the near term, HR professionals will continue to grapple with the effects of increased health care costs, continuing globalization and retiring baby boomers. SHRM research suggests that many routine HR functions will be outsourced and sent offshore, enabling HR professionals to concentrate on more strategic priorities.

When asked about how the HR profession has changed, HR volunteer leaders generally agree that HR has made great strides in becoming more strategic and less transactional. "Early in my career, the scope of the human resource role was very narrow—very process-oriented. We were considered to be more of a function rather than a resource," recalls Janet Parker, SPHR, 2007–2008 Board chair. "Now we are much more than a function. We are recognized as HR experts, and we add value at all levels in our organizations—domestically and internationally. Now there is a recognition of HR's role, and there is definitely increased credibility that the profession has gained throughout the years."

Long-time SHRM member and volunteer leader Pat Miller agrees. The 37-year HR veteran notes that "the changes are as acute as the generation that lived through the first flight of the Wright Brothers to flight evolving for mail and war bomb delivery. I started as a personnel director directly out of college for a manufacturing firm with 250 employees. I was the first woman in management with grandiose ideas of what I wanted to accomplish. The first day, I opened the door to my office and found it littered with applications and a list of 20 positions I was to fill ASAP. I was the HR department and didn't have a computer much less the Internet to find answers. I dove in headfirst, and through sheer perseverance, I did not drown. With turnover more than 100 percent and every organization in town hiring, I needed to get creative fast. Through compressed workweeks to new-hire Friday afternoon parties—activities that seem everyday strategies today—I managed to get the lone woman's voice heard. Feeding managers what they are hungry for rather than what I wanted to cook is a lesson I learned early."

SHRM volunteer Peter Bye agrees and adds that technology and diversity have also changed the HR profession over the past 20 years. "The pace, scope and dynamic nature of business have evolved dramatically over the past 20 years. Along with this, we have seen changes in technology that could not have been contemplated 20 years ago. The primary effect on the HR profession is the ever-increasing 'bar' of what it takes to be relevant to an organization and to truly help shape the organization's future. HR professionals must leverage technology, learn the business in which their organization is engaged and continually adapt their priorities. ... Today, organizations also routinely deal with greater levels of cultural diversity every day. This holds true regardless of whether the organization is located entirely within one small geographic area or globally in 180 countries. Today's HR professionals must be culturally competent to work in and help guide such a workplace."

With all the positive changes in the profession, though, many agree that ultimately, HR's place in an organization is still up to the individual. Parker notes that "SHRM can provide the best of everything, but individuals need to make the decision at the level they want to work. Continuous learning is critical for HR professionals. SHRM has consistently provided us with the tools that are not only relevant for what we do today but also for what we will be doing in the future. Having the right tools is important; however, how we use those tools will determine our credibility and success."

Former SHRM President and CEO Susan Meisinger, SPHR, agrees. The outsourcing and offshoring of routine HR functions will result in fewer HR professionals with higher skill levels. "HR helps run the business," notes Meisinger. "The focus is increasingly on talent management—finding, keeping and leveraging that talent to meet organizational goals. Those HR professionals who aren't at that level may not make it in tomorrow's workplace." HR has moved beyond the routine transaction level, and those who are

not willing to become strategic partners may just be left behind. Former SHRM President and CEO Michael Losey, SPHR, summed up Meisinger's and Parker's assertions by saying, "It's not that we need more HR people; we need better HR people."

SHRM's long-term initiatives reflect the Society's mission to "Serve the Professional" and "Advance the Profession." Internationalization efforts (establishing offices and programs in India and China) reflect the increased globalization and diversity of the workplace. SHRM's early and continued involvement in diversity has made the association a leader in diversity management, and the academic initiative reflects the Society's position to better prepare those entering the field.

ASPA's founders formed the Society to promote and elevate the standards and performance of the profession, to provide data and information to its members, and to gain recognition of the value of the field. SHRM will continue the founders' vision but in ways few could have imagined in 1948. As we celebrate our past, we know that our work has just started.

The next 60 years of SHRM and the profession are going to be even more challenging and radically different from what we've seen before—but just like the past 60 years, SHRM will be with its members at every stage, providing opportunities and helping them meet the new demands of business.

"HR helps run the business. The focus is increasingly on talent management— finding, keeping and leveraging that talent to meet organizational goals. Those HR professionals who aren't at that level may not make it in tomorrow's workplace."

— Sue Meisinger, SPHR

SHRM Survey on How HR Has Changed in the Past 10 Years

SHRM recently asked volunteers for their perceptions on how HR has changed in the past 10 years. Eighty-seven percent of respondents said that the growing importance of managing health care costs for organizations had a significant effect on the profession. Sixty percent of respondents noted that the need to effectively manage an organization's talent was a major change, and 58 percent noted the increased role of HR in an organization's strategic planning process. Issues that have changed HR include:

The Human Resource Function

n –342	Significant impact	Moderate impact	Minor/ no impact
Growing importance of health care cost management for companies	87%	13%	1%
Growing importance of talent management in relation to business strategy	60%	36%	4%
Increased HR role in organization's strategic planning	58%	38%	4%
Increased access to self-service HR resources by employees and to applications by job candidates	52%	40%	8%
Increased global human capital management responsibilities through the expansion of multinational operations and the use of offshoring	41%	38%	21%
Development of new roles for HR departments, such as ethics management and corporate social responsibility	37%	45%	18%
Increased use of human resource management outsourcing	29%	49%	22%
Consolidation and competition changing the HR consulting/outsourcing industry	23%	54%	23%

Note: Data sorted in descending order by the "Significant impact" column. Percentages are row percentages and may not total 100% due to rounding.

SHRM **Leadership**

Lon O'Neil
Chief Executive Officer

China Gorman
Chief Operating Officer

SHRM Board **Chairs**

Janet N. Parker, SPHR
2007–2008

Johnny C. Taylor, Jr., J.D.,
SPHR
2005–2006

David B. Hutchins, SPHR,
CEBS, CCP
2003–2004

Ommy Strauch, SPHR
2002

Libby Sartain, SPHR, CCP
2001

Michael J. Lotito, SPHR
2000

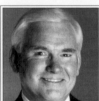

Gary L. Howard, SPHR
1999

Kathleen McComber, SPHR
1998

Neal D. Bondy, SPHR
1997

Bruce R. Ellig, SPHR
1996

Kenneth Ranftle, SPHR
1995

Gail E. Aldrich, SPHR
1994

Elmer C. Jackson III, SPHR
1993

Charles E. Gallagher, SPHR
1992

Kathryn D. McKee, SPHR, CCP
1991

SHRM Board **Chairs**

Wanda A. Lee, SPHR,
CCP, MCO
1990

Thomas G. Kelley, SPHR
1989

James G. Parkel, SPHR
1988

Merle T. Alvis, SPHR
1987

Richard J. Messer, SPHR
1986

Irene H. Florida, SPHR
1985

James H. Skaggs, SPHR
1984

James E. Ware, SPHR
1983

John L. Quigley, AEP
1982

Jerry L. Sellentin, Ph.D., AEP
1981

Thomas B. Burke, AEP
1980

John D. Blodger, AEP
1979

Zean Jamison Jr., AEP
1978

Rudolph H. Weber, AEP
1977

Russell G. Williams, AEP
1976

George A. Rieder
1975

Wilson L. Nicoll, AEP
1974

William B. Pardue, AEP
1973

Clyde Benedict, AEP
1972

Frank Plasha
1971

SHRM Board **Chairs**

Drew M. Young, AEP
1970

Donald B. Roark
1969

Robert L. Berra, AEP
1968

Wiley I. Beavers, AEP
1967

Edward J. Henry, AEP
1966

Virgil S. Hanson
1965

George J. Trombold, APD
1964

Paul E. Jacobs
1963

Theo K. Mitchelson
1962

David W. Harris
1961

SHRM Board **Chairs**

Jack Linzie
1960

Earl D. McConnell
1959

Bert M. Walter
1958

Marshall J. Diebold
1957

Leonard R. Brice, AEP
1956

Paul E. Hensel
1955

L. Reed Clark
1954

Russell L. Moberly, APD
1953

Leonard J. Smith, APD
1952

Walter C. Mason
1948–1951